# ART AT AUCTION 1984–85

**Jean-Baptiste-Camille Corot**
WOMAN IN A TOQUE WITH A MANDOLIN
Signed, *circa* 1850–55, 44in by 34⅝in (111.8cm by 88cm)
New York $3,850,000 (£3,007,813). 14.XI.84
From the collection of Mr and Mrs David Bakalar

# ART AT AUCTION
## The year at Sotheby's 1984–85

SOTHEBY'S PUBLICATIONS

© Sotheby's 1985

First published for Sotheby's Publications by
Philip Wilson Publishers Ltd,
Russell Chambers, Covent Garden, London WC2E 8AA
and
Sotheby's Publications,
Harper & Row, Publishers, Inc.,
10 East 53rd Street, New York, NY 10022

ISBN 0 85667 303 X
ISSN 0084–6783
Library of Congress Catalog Card Number 67 30652

Editor: Georgia Fogg
Assistants: Louise Berg, Susan Morris
Assistant (New York): Elizabeth White

Design: Mary Osborne
Printed in England by Jolly & Barber Ltd, Rugby, Warwickshire,
and bound by Dorstel Press Ltd, Harlow, Essex

*Note*
Prices given throughout this book include the buyer's premium
applicable in the saleroom concerned. These prices are shown in
the currency in which they were realised. The sterling and dollar
equivalent figures, shown in brackets, are for guidance only and
are based on the rounded rates of exchange on 1 June 1985. These
rates for each pound sterling are as follows: Australian dollars,
1.93; Hong Kong dollars, 10.00; United States dollars, 1.28;
French francs, 12.00; Swiss francs, 3.31; Dutch guilders, 4.43;
Italian lire, 2,510; Spanish pesetas, 223.00; South African rand,
2.56.

Sotheby's galleries at Bond Street, Bloomfield Place and
Conduit Street are indicated by the designation 'London',
and those at York Avenue by the designation 'New York'.

*Endpaper*
**Jan Brandes**
*An elephant-trapping kraal in Colombo, Ceylon, December 1785*, two views from a portfolio of over
400 watercolours and drawings recording travels in Java, Ceylon and the Cape of Good Hope,
1784–86, $6\frac{1}{4}$in by $7\frac{7}{8}$in (16cm by 20cm)
London £55,000 ($70,400). 2.V.85

# Contents

A Benin bronze memorial head of an Oba, Nigeria, *circa* fourteenth century, height 8⅝in (22cm)
London £352,000 ($450,560). 24.VI.85

# Preface

A. Alfred Taubman
Chairman, Sotheby's Holdings

The events of the 1984–85 auction season dramatically illustrate the international character of the art market, a market that has expanded substantially, with many new collectors present in our salerooms. We welcome their participation and have concentrated on developing an increased international presence for Sotheby's, while broadening our services, the better to accommodate our clients world-wide.

One example of this commitment was the auction of the Gould Collection of paintings and drawings in New York. Forty of the most important Impressionist works from the collection were exhibited in Tokyo, London, and Lausanne, giving European and Japanese collectors a unique opportunity to view the paintings. Equal excitement was generated in New York, reflected in the sale total of $34 million, the highest ever achieved for a private collection of fine art.

Many of the paintings from the Gould Collection are illustrated in this edition of *Art at Auction*, which presents a beautiful visual review of the highlights of the year at Sotheby's: a Fabergé Imperial Easter egg; a magnificent silver dinner service by Paul de Lamerie; a rediscovered masterpiece by Guido Reni and many other exquisite works of art that have passed through our salerooms around the world.

During the year, new offices were opened in Singapore and Tel Aviv and special auctions were held in Geneva and Jerusalem, coinciding with important cultural events in those cities. In addition, we are expanding our educational programs in the United States and introducing new financial services on both sides of the Atlantic.

Special thanks must go to the members of the Board of Directors of Sotheby's Holdings, whose guidance, diligence and support are essential to our efforts. We are particularly fortunate during the 1984–85 auction season to have HRH the Infanta Pilar de Borbon, Duchess of Badajoz, join the Board. I take great personal pride in my association with this unique group of distinguished and talented individuals.

The development and implementation of our international programs are, in large measure, the achievement of Michael L. Ainslie, President and Chief Executive Officer of Sotheby's Holdings. Michael assumed this role at the beginning of the 1984–85 season, which has been the most profitable in Sotheby's 241-year history. With the Board and the experts of Sotheby's world-wide, I salute the accomplishments of his first year and look forward to the future with confidence.

The Cuckoo Egg, a Fabergé gold, enamel and jewelled Imperial Easter egg with singing bird automaton, workmaster Mikhail Perchin, St Petersburg, 1900, height 8in (20.3cm)
New York $1,760,000 (£1,375,000). 11.VI.85
From the collection of Mr and Mrs Bernard C. Solomon

Fifty-four Easter eggs were commissioned from Fabergé by Alexander III and Nicholas II of Russia. This Easter gift, called the Cuckoo Egg, was the first of six automaton eggs that he created between 1900 and 1911.

# Paintings and drawings

**Giovanni Bellini**
A MASTER AND HIS PUPIL
On panel, 17½in by 25in (44.5cm by 63.5cm)
New York $484,000 (£378,125). 6.VI.85

*Opposite*
**Cenni di Francesco**
THE VIRGIN AND CHILD ENTHRONED WITH SAINTS AND ANGELS: THE RISEN CHRIST FLANKED BY THE VIRGIN
AND SAINT JOHN (in the predella)
Tempera on gold ground on panel, 34¼in by 18⅞in (87cm by 48cm)
London £143,000 ($183,040). 3.VII.85

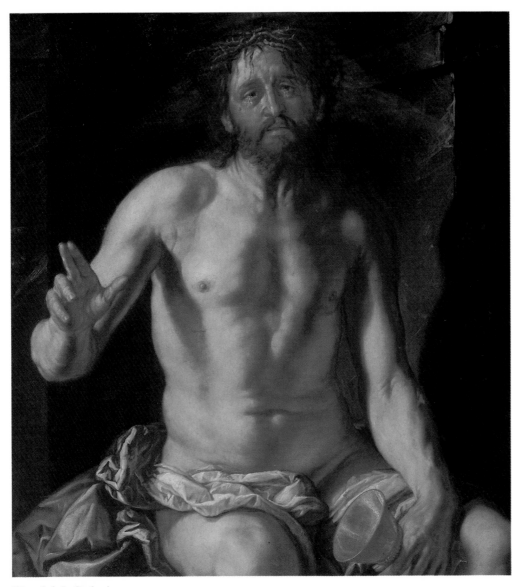

**Hendrick Goltzius**
CHRIST THE REDEEMER
On panel, signed with monogram and dated *1613*, 33½in by 27½in (85cm by 70cm)
London £132,000 ($168,960). 3.VII.85

*Opposite*
**Lucas Cranach the Elder**
HERCULES BETWEEN VIRTUE AND VICE
On panel, signed with the winged serpent, 25in by 17¾in (63.5cm by 45cm)
London £264,000 ($337,920). 3.IV.85

# *David with the head of Goliath* by Guido Reni

## John Somerville

On 3 April 1985 an unknown and unrecorded painting by Guido Reni (1575–1642) of *David with the head of Goliath* (Fig. 1), was sold in London for £2,200,000. This price would not have been so remarkable were it not for the fact that another version of the same composition was known. Now hanging in the Louvre in Paris (Fig. 2), that picture had, for centuries, been a celebrated work of the artist.

The authenticity of the Louvre painting had never been doubted, but the appearance of the Sotheby's picture immediately set scholars and art historians thinking about the dating of both paintings. Whereas the Louvre version had always been ascribed to Reni's early period and dated to *circa* 1605–1606, the London picture was clearly a more mature work, of a style and technique quite different from the other version. The eminent Reni scholar, Dr D. Stephen Pepper, dates the Sotheby's painting to *circa* 1618–20. This dating is supported not only by the powerful drawing, broad and assured brushwork and the delicate palette, but by comparison with other works of this period. In addition, Carlo Cesare Malvasia in his life of Guido Reni (1678) mentions the *David* when discussing a group of paintings that generally belong to the early 1620s.

The question of dating is complicated further by the fact that Malvasia also speaks of Reni's *David* as being a companion to a *Judith with the head of Holofernes* (Sedlmeyer Collection, Geneva), dated by Pepper to the mid-1620s. The dimensions of the *Judith* are almost identical to those of the *David* sold by Sotheby's, while the Paris picture is taller. Pepper's dating is not supported by documentation, and it is possible that, despite the similarity in size, the two paintings were not conceived as a pair but were later hung as pendants, due to their subject matter. An additional factor that has a bearing on the dating of the *David* was the publication in 1619 of G.B. Marino's *La Galleria*, in which he dedicated a sonnet to Reni's *David*. It would seem more likely that this sonnet was inspired by the Sotheby's picture, which, on stylistic grounds, can be considered to be contemporaneous. But if the Sotheby's *David* is closer to the *Judith* in date, that is after, rather than before 1620, then the poem must refer back to the Louvre *David*. Later in his biography, Malvasia refers to 'Davids' but he makes no claim that they were identical in composition. Indeed, all that he alludes to is the model for the *Davids*, one Cavaliere Bellini, and the features of yet another *David* in Vienna, of quite different composition, are certainly similar to those of the Paris and Sotheby's *Davids*.

Fig. 1
**Guido Reni**
DAVID WITH THE HEAD OF GOLIATH
84⅜in by 56¼in (214.5cm by 143cm)
London £2,200,000 ($2,816,000). 3.IV.85

As one of the most powerful and arresting images in Italian baroque painting, Reni's magnificent composition must have had a considerable impact, whether it was executed *circa* 1605 or *circa* 1620. This is borne out by the numerous imitations and copies that were made, both at the time and in the centuries to follow. Although there are differences between the Louvre and the Sotheby's paintings: the angle of David's head, the size and features of Goliath's head, the length of the pelt and the position of the sling, they are essentially the same. So why should Reni have wanted to repeat himself? Certainly by 1620 Caravaggio's style, with which the young Reni had had a short-lived flirtation, was losing favour and, indeed, Reni and his followers came to consider it a degenerate art form, suited only to 'low-life' subjects. Should we therefore see the second version as a kind of apologia? If the Louvre *David* can be seen as Reni's most slavish imitation of Caravaggio, then it is not impossible that at a later stage in his career, established as one of the greatest painters of the age, he felt the need to reject once and for all those influences, and possibly wanted to show how this powerful image could and should be handled.

The one fact that cannot be doubted in all this is that the Sotheby's picture is an infinitely more accomplished and sensitive work. The images have been refined, especially in the subtle way in which David's head is turned from profile to three-quarter face, giving the giant-slayer a more compassionate rather than a cruel, sneering air. The broad and masterly brushwork, the self-assured way in which the artist has delineated the shapes and defined the volume of David's body so that the weight is transmitted down the right leg, resting securely on its foot, confirmed, even without cleaning, the authorship of Guido Reni himself. There is not this brilliance in the Paris picture where, for example, the right elbow hovers unsatisfactorily above the column. In the Sotheby's painting, the problem has been resolved by the tilting back of David's head, which requires the right shoulder to be hunched ever so slightly, but which in turn draws the elbow down to rest securely upon the column. The tight yet coarse execution of the Louvre picture can perhaps be explained not only by the influence of Caravaggio but by the artist's relative inexperience, though it has to be admitted that some other works from this period are more accomplished. The Louvre painting has a layer of heavily discoloured varnish and until this is removed and it can be examined closely, its precise dating and indeed its true status cannot really be determined. By the time the Sotheby's *David* was painted, Reni was at the height of his powers and it was not perhaps until the 1630s, after his recovery from a mental breakdown, that his genius was again to be realised.

But what is the history of the Sotheby's painting? How is it possible that such a great masterpiece could have disappeared from view? There is no simple answer. Pierre-Jean Mariette, in his *Abecedario*, states that the version now in the Louvre was still in Bologna when the artist painted the second version, which was, he continues, in the collection of Prince Eugene of Savoy. But this claim was made at least one hundred years after the execution of either version, with the advantage of hindsight, and without reference to Malvasia, whose life of Reni is the most comprehensive information we have about his work.

Fig. 2
**Guido Reni**
DAVID WITH THE HEAD OF GOLIATH
*Circa* 1605–1606, 106¼in by 66⅞in
(270cm by 170cm)
Reproduced courtesy of the
Louvre, Paris

Malvasia stated that the *David* had gone into the collection of the King of France, but he then admitted that this was only hearsay. Since the Louvre painting was first recorded in the French Royal Collection in 1706, it has always been considered to be the work Malvasia referred to, in the absence until now of any other claimant. There was, however, the painting of the same composition in Prince Eugene's collection and this could have been the picture that re-emerged at Sotheby's. But it was this very obscurity that had allowed such a great painting to escape the attention not only of art historians but of restorers. Now that it has been cleaned it is shown to be in a marvellous state of preservation. The overall silver tonality, the paint applied with a brilliant feathery touch over a warm red ground confirm that this painting is one of Reni's greatest works.

**Sir Peter Paul Rubens**
THE MARTYRDOM OF ST URSULA AND HER MAIDENS
On panel, *circa* 1615–20, 25¼in by 19½in (64cm by 49.5cm)
London £429,000 ($549,120). 3.IV.85

**Sir Peter Paul Rubens**
THE LAST SUPPER
On panel, *circa* 1632, 24¼in by 19⅛in (61.5cm by 48.5cm)
London £374,000 ($478,720). 12.XII.84
From the collection of Peter Mertens

This grisaille is the model for an engraving by Boëtius à Bolswert. Rubens painted an altarpiece
of similar composition for the church of St Rombout at Malines, which is now in the Brera Gallery,
Milan.

**Philippe de Champaigne**

PORTRAIT OF LOUIS XIII
Titled, inscribed *LPD* and numbered *P105*<sup>bis</sup> on the reverse, branded with the collector's mark of
Louis-Philippe, *L·P·D*, on the stretcher 28¼in by 23¼in (71.7cm by 59cm)
New York $159,500 (£124,609). 17.I.85

**Nicolas Mignard called Mignard d'Avignon**
VENUS AND ADONIS
107⅜in by 69⅝in (273cm by 177cm)
Monte Carlo FF1,387,500 (£115,625:$148,079). 8.XII.84

**Carel Fabritius**
MERCURY AND ARGUS
Signed, 28⅞in by 41in (73.5cm by 104cm)
Monte Carlo FF7,992,000 (£666,000:$852,935). 22.VI.85

**Pieter Lastman**
HAGAR AND THE ANGEL
On panel, signed with monogram and dated *1614*, 20in by 26⅞in (51cm by 68.3cm)
New York $253,000 (£197,656). 6.VI.85
From the collection of Mr and Mrs Bernard Solomon

Pieter Lastman was one of the most important painters in Amsterdam in the early seventeenth century, and was influential in his use of Biblical texts as the subjects of his pictures. This was reflected in the work of the young Rembrandt, who studied with Lastman in 1623.

**Pieter Brueghel the Younger**
SPRING
On panel, signed and dated *1635*, 17⅛in by 23in (43.5cm by 58.3cm)
Amsterdam Dfl997,600 (£225,192:$288,324). 26.XI.84

**Pieter Brueghel the Younger**
A WEDDING FEAST
On panel, signed, 45¼in by 67¾in (115cm by 172cm)
London £660,000 ($844,800). 12.XII.84

**Salomon van Ruysdael**
A RIVER LANDSCAPE WITH BOATS AND A CHATEAU
On panel, signed with monogram and dated *1645*, 24¾in by 36¼in (63cm by 92cm)
London £363,000 ($464,640). 3.VII.85

*Opposite*
**Jan Van Os**
STILL LIFE OF FLOWERS, FRUIT AND A BIRD'S NEST ON A MARBLE LEDGE
On panel, signed, 34½in by 27in (87.5cm by 68.6cm)
New York $253,000 (£197,656). 17.I.85

**Frans Post**
VIEW OVER THE VARZEA, BRAZIL
On panel, signed and dated *1667*, 17½in by 21¾in (44.5cm by 55.3cm)
New York $330,000 (£257,813). 17.I.85
From the collection of the Herbert F. Johnson Museum of Art, Cornell University

*Opposite*
**Francisco José de Goya y Lucientes**
THE DUCHESS OF ALBA AND HER DUENNA
Signed and dated *1795*, 12in by 9⅞in (30.5cm by 25cm)
Madrid Ptas 50,600,000 (£226,906:$290,805). 27.II.85

*Left*
**Jacopo Carucci called Pontormo**
STUDY OF A STANDING MALE NUDE, LEANING FORWARDS
Black chalk heightened with white chalk, squared in black and
red chalk; a red chalk study of the same figure on the reverse,
*circa* 1514–19, 13¾in by 7¾in (35cm by 19.6cm)
New York $143,000 (£111,719). 16.I.85

*Opposite*
**Hendrick Goltzius**
MARS AND VENUS SURPRISED BY JUPITER IN THE FORGE OF VULCAN
Pen and brown ink and wash heightened with white over
black chalk, 16¼in by 12¼in (41.4cm by 31.2cm)
Amsterdam DFl719,200 (£162,348:$207,861). 26.XI.84

This is a study in reverse for Goltzius' engraving dated 1585.

*Below*
**Francesco dei Rossi called Il Salviati**
STUDY OF A RECLINING MALE NUDE
Red chalk heightened with white chalk, 10½in by 15½in
(26.8cm by 39.5cm)
London £101,200 ($129,536). 4.VII.85

**Hendrick Avercamp**
ICE SCENE WITH A GENTLEMAN ADMIRING A LADY IN THE FOREGROUND, KOLF PLAYERS BEYOND
Black chalk, grey wash, watercolour and gouache, signed with monogram,
7¾in by 12⅜in (19.6cm by 31.6cm)
Amsterdam Dfl220,400 (£49,752:$63,699). 26.XI.84

**Jan van Goyen**
A VILLAGE FESTIVAL WITH MUSICIANS PLAYING OUTSIDE A TENT
Black chalk and grey wash, signed with initials and dated *1653*, 6⅝in by 10⅞in (17cm by 27.7cm)
Amsterdam Dfl92,800 (£20,948:$26,821). 26.XI.84

**Pierre-Joseph Redouté**
TULIPS AND ROSES
Watercolour on vellum, signed and dated *an XI*, 19⅛in by 14in (48.6cm by 35.7cm)
Monte Carlo FF1,221,000 (£101,750:$130,309). 22.VI.85

**Nathaniel Dance, RA**
PORTRAIT OF THOMAS ASSHETON-SMITH
Signed and dated *1775*, 92½in by 55⅞in (235cm by 142cm)
London £83,600 ($107,008). 13.III.85

**Bartholomew Dandridge**
EQUESTRIAN PORTRAIT OF CAPTAIN
RICHARD GIFFORD
Signed, 48in by 38in (122cm by 96.5cm)
London £39,600 ($50,688). 10.VII.85

**Sir Henry Raeburn, RA**
MASTER WILLIAM BLAIR OF AVONTOUN
*Circa* 1814, 29½in by 24¼in (75cm by 61.5cm)
New York $148,500 (£116,016). 25.IV.85
From the collection of the late Florence J. Gould

**Sir Joshua Reynolds, PRA**
PORTRAIT OF MISS HARVEY
Inscribed on the reverse *Mifs Harvey/*
*painted by Sir Joshua Reynolds/1789,*
22in by 16½in (56cm by 42cm)
London £82,500 ($105,600). 21.XI.84

**Philip Mercier**
PORTRAIT OF A BOY
Signed and dated *1740*, 50in by 40in
(127cm by 101.5cm)
London £41,800 ($53,504). 21.XI.84
From the collection of the late
Mrs M.A.L. Williams

**John Constable, RA**
FLATFORD MILL
*Circa* 1813–17, 9½in by 7¼in (24cm by 18.5cm)
London £121,000 ($154,880). 13.III.85

*Opposite*
**John Constable, RA**
THE LAMBERT CHILDREN
1825, 23in by 18¾in (58.5cm by 47.5cm)
London £242,000 ($309,760). 13.III.85

**John Wootton**
TWO OF THE DUCHESS OF MARLBOROUGH'S DOGS
Signed and dated *1736*, 65in by 70½in (165cm by 179cm)
London £143,000 ($183,040). 10.VII.85
From the collection of the Earl Spencer, MVO

This painting was commissioned by Sarah, Duchess of Marlborough for her house at Windsor and was inherited by her favourite grandson, the Honourable John Spencer.

## John Wootton
A BAY RACEHORSE, THE PROPERTY OF RICHARD SMYTH, ESQ., BEING HELD BY A GROOM AND WITH HOUNDS
Signed and dated *1737*, 89½in by 139¼in (227.5cm by 353cm)
London £269,500 ($344,960). 13.III.85

**Ben Marshall**
TOM OLDAKER ON A GREY HUNTER, WITH HUNTSMEN AND HOUNDS IN A LANDSCAPE
36in by 48in (91.5cm by 122cm)
New York $176,000 (£137,500). 6.VI.85
From the collection of F. William Carr

*Opposite*
**Richard Roper**
THE KNOX SPORTING SCREEN
Signed and dated *A.D. 1759*, the front comprising twelve paintings of hunting subjects, and on the
reverse eighteen portraits of celebrated racehorses with riders and grooms,
106in by 144in (269cm by 366cm)
London £247,500 ($316,800). 10.VII.85

**Thomas Rowlandson**
PLACE DES VICTOIRES, PARIS
Pen and grey ink and watercolour over pencil, *circa* 1783, 14⅛in by 20¾in (36cm by 52.7cm)
London £93,500 ($119,680). 14.III.85

This watercolour, engraved and published in November 1789, just four months after the storming of the Bastille, highlights the decadence of French society in the years before the French Revolution. Beyond the Place des Victoires Rowlandson introduced the twin towers of Notre Dame, in reality some distance away, to help the English viewer recognise without doubt that the setting is Paris.

*Opposite*
**Sir Thomas Lawrence,** PRA
PORTRAIT OF COUNTESS CZERNIN
Coloured chalks heightened with white on prepared canvas, *circa* 1818–19,
33½in by 27¾in (85cm by 70.5cm)
London £23,100 ($29,568). 11.VII.85
From the collection of Graf und Gräfin Emil von Spannocchi

**William Callow,** RWS
PONT ROYAL, PARIS
Watercolour over pencil with bodycolour and scratching out, signed and dated *1839*,
9¼in by 12¾in (23.5cm by 32.5cm)
London £25,300 ($32,384). 14.III.85

*Opposite, above*
**Joseph Mallord William Turner,** RA
VIEW OF AN ALPINE TOWN
Pen, black ink and red ink with watercolour over pencil on blue paper, *circa* 1830–33,
5½in by 7½in (14cm by 19cm)
London £41,800 ($53,504). 14.III.85
From the collection of Mrs C.H. Tattersall

*Opposite, below*
**Joseph Mallord William Turner,** RA
BONNEVILLE, SAVOY
Watercolour, *circa* 1807, 11in by 15in (28cm by 38cm)
London £110,000 ($140,800). 21.XI.84

This is the first of three watercolour versions of the same composition based on a sketch from Turner's
1802 Alpine tour. It was commissioned by Walter Fawkes *circa* 1807.

### Charles Robert Cockerell, RA

A TRIBUTE TO SIR CHRISTOPHER WREN

Watercolour over pencil heightened with bodycolour with scratching out, inscribed on a label on the backboard *A Tribute to the memory of Sir Christopher Wren/being a collection of the principal Works/. . . ector si monumentum requisis/Circumspice/C. R. Cockerell Arch R.A.*, 39in by 52in (99cm by 132cm)
London £49,500 ($63,360). 23.V.85

C.R. Cockerell, Surveyor of St Paul's Cathedral from 1819, made this imaginary perspective of Wren's major works as a tribute to the architect he considered 'the patriarch of a great race'.

*Opposite*

### Emily Lefroy

Two views from a volume of watercolours of Bermuda and Canada, 1871–79
London £24,200 ($30,976). 8.XI.84

The views of Bermuda were drawn during the governorship of Sir John Henry Lefroy (1871–77) by members of the Governor's family and friends.

**Daniel Maclise,** ARA
HARRIET LOUISA AND MARIA, DAUGHTERS OF FREDERICK MILLETT
Signed, 24in by 20in (61cm by 50.8cm)
London £44,000($56,320). 27.XI.84

**George Frederic Watts, OM, RA**
ENDYMION
*Circa* 1872, 20½in by 25½in (52cm by 65cm)
London £110,000 ($140,800). 18.VI.85

**James-Jacques-Joseph Tissot**
A YOUNG GIRL IN A BOAT
Signed, 1870, 19¾in by 25⅝in (50cm by 65cm)
London £341,500($437,120). 18.VI.85

This painting was exhibited at the Paris Salon in 1870 as *Jeune femme en bateau*.

*Opposite*
**James-Jacques-Joseph Tissot**
ON THE THAMES (RETURN FROM HENLEY)
Signed, *circa* 1883–85, 57¾in by 40in (146.7cm by 101.6cm)
New York $407,000 (£317,969). 23.V.85
From the collection of Newark Museum, New Jersey

**Sir Edward John Poynter, Bt, PRA**
CHLOE, DULCES DOCTA MODOS ET CITHARAE SCIENS
Signed with monogram and dated *1893*, 28in by 36in (71cm by 91.5cm)
London £220,000($281,600). 18.VI.85

This painting was exhibited at the Royal Academy in 1893. The title, from Horace's *Odes*, reads,
'Chloë, skilled in sweet measures and mistress of the lyre.'

*Opposite*
**John William Waterhouse, RA**
THISBE or THE LISTENER
Signed and dated *1909*, 38¼in by 23¼in (97cm by 59cm)
London £93,500($119,680). 18.VI.85

This painting was exhibited at the Royal Academy in 1909.

**Edward Robert Hughes, RWS**

HEART OF SNOW

Watercolour and bodycolour, signed, and signed and titled on a label on the backboard,
29½in by 44½in (75cm by 113cm)
London £15,400($19,712). 17.X.84

**Edward Atkinson Hornel**
THE SHAWL
Signed and dated '95, 24in by 24in (61cm by 61cm)
Hopetoun House £20,900($26,752). 30.IV.85

**Sir George Clausen, RA**
SCHOOLGIRLS, HAVERSTOCK HILL
Signed and dated *1880*, 20in by 29$\frac{7}{8}$in (51cm by 76cm)
London £42,900 ($54,912). 15.V.85
From the collection of the late Colonel C.Michael Paul

Clausen's bold composition creates an impression of a sudden encounter with the schoolgirls, an effect remarked upon in a number of contemporary reviews. In 1880 *The Times* critic commented: '...Some of them, indeed, have almost escaped from the frame, it seems, since the figures are cut off about the middle of their dresses. The first feeling about this picture is an angry one – that the artist should make all his damsels' features so blunt and indefinite in outline, and their complexions of such purply tinge ... if, however, we forget these demerits what a fresh charming little picture it is! ...'

*Opposite*
**Walter Osborne, RHA**
BOYS ON THE QUAY
Signed and dated *'84*, 24in by 20in (61cm by 51cm)
London £39,600 ($50,688). 15.V.85

# *Virginia Woolf* by Vanessa Bell

## Richard Shone

> I have just refused to sit for my portrait for the Nat. Portrait Gallery; dont you
> agree I am right? They send a wretched boy to draw one in one sitting; then they
> keep the drawing in a cellar, and when I've been dead ten years they have it out
> and say Does anyone want to know what Mrs Woolf looked like? No, say all the
> others. Then its torn up. So why should I defile a whole day by sitting?

It is well known that Virginia Woolf disliked sitting for her portrait; this surely is the
real reason behind her refusal, amusingly recounted above in a letter to Quentin Bell
of 15 February 1934, to be 'done' for the National Portrait Gallery. She had earlier
refused to sit to David Bomberg; she denied Cecil Beaton more than once. When she
agreed to sit to the sculptor Stephen Tomlin in 1931 she seems to have forgotten her
horror of being peered at and scrutinised; it soon returned, however, and after six
short sittings the venture was abandoned. She writes a bitter passage in her *Diary* on
24 June 1939 about being tricked into sitting to the French photographer Gisèle
Freund, of how an afternoon was to be wasted in the 'most detestable and upsetting'
way of all. Tomlin's head and shoulders is, however, in her biographer's words, 'far
more like than any of the photographs'.

In spite of her reluctance, several portraits of Virginia Woolf exist. Among them
are four paintings from 1912 by her sister Vanessa Bell (Figs 1, 2, 3 and 4) and one by
Roger Fry. Two of the four Bell portraits were auctioned at Sotheby's this past
season; Figure 1 was sold last year and Figure 3 was in the saleroom in May. Almost
nothing is known of the circumstances of these studies but it seems likely that they
were painted at Asheham House, Sussex, which Virginia Woolf rented from February
1912. Before that she had taken Little Talland House in Firle village; it is possible
that Figure 4 was painted there. Obviously Figure 1 was a formal sitting. Roger Fry
painted the writer on the same occasion, producing a frontal portrait, which, if less
fluently handled, perhaps has more psychological insight.

Both the paintings sold at Sotheby's seem to have been done over a short period
of time. Their small size suggests a weekend visit rather than sittings in London.
Fry visited Asheham more than once in the spring of 1912, though Figure 1 seems
to belong stylistically to Vanessa Bell's work of later in the year. The assured
simplicity of handling and the light yet subdued colour are characteristic of her first

Fig. 1
**Vanessa Bell**
PORTRAIT OF VIRGINIA WOOLF
On board, 1912, 15¾in by 11⅜in (39cm by 29cm)
London £16,500 ($21,120). 14.XI.84
From the collection of Mrs Trekkie Parsons

Fig. 2
**Vanessa Bell**
VIRGINIA WOOLF AT ASHEHAM
1912, 14½in by 12in
(36.8cm by 30.5cm)
Photograph reproduced courtesy of
the Anthony d'Offay Gallery, London

Post-Impressionist pictures. They show Virginia Woolf in the year of her marriage to Leonard Woolf, before she had published any fiction and before the devastating breakdown of 1913, which considerably altered her looks.

Figure 3 was more than likely painted in the garden at Asheham, or at least on the terrace, which ran the length of the house. It belongs to a group of portraits and figure studies of 1912 in which Vanessa Bell omits facial detail in her search for simplicity and clear form, yet this image of Virginia Woolf in a deck-chair is instantly recognisable. The present writer recollects looking at the painting when it hung at Monk's House and Leonard Woolf and Duncan Grant both agreed that it was 'astonishingly like Virginia'.

It is surely a matter of regret that the three artists in Virginia Woolf's circle, Roger Fry, Duncan Grant and Vanessa Bell, did not contrive situations in which she could have been induced to sit for them more frequently, but, as her published diary makes

Fig. 3
**Vanessa Bell**
VIRGINIA WOOLF IN A DECK-CHAIR
On board, 1912, 14in by 9½in (35.5cm by 24cm)
London £19,800 ($25,344). 15.V.85
From the collection of Mrs Trekkie Parsons

Fig. 4
**Vanessa Bell**
VIRGINIA WOOLF
1912, 16in by 12in
(40.7cm by 30.5cm)
Photograph reproduced
courtesy of the Anthony
d'Offay Gallery, London

clear, her life between the wars was extraordinarily busy. When Vanessa Bell wished to paint her sister in the early 1930s, the only other occasion that she did so, she had to take her easel, paints and canvas to Tavistock Square while Virginia Woolf sat reading manuscripts (admittedly Lady Ottoline Morrell's memoirs were among them, which considerably enlivened the proceedings). Down in Sussex, the inhabitants of Monk's House and of Charleston would usually only meet for lunch or tea at weekends. As soon as she noticed she was being drawn surreptitiously, Virginia Woolf would become self-conscious and, as Duncan Grant ruefully admitted, 'might get up and walk out of the room'. So we must be particularly thankful for these two beautiful images of her which mark more carefree days.

**Christopher Richard Wynne Nevinson, ARA**
TEMPLES OF NEW YORK
Signed, 1919, 26in by 16in
(66cm by 40.5cm)
London £30,800
($39,424). 14.XI.84

This view of Trinity
Church, Wall Street was
painted in London after
Nevinson's return from his
first trip to New York in
1919.

**William Roberts, RA**
TRAFALGAR SQUARE
1926, 30in by 36in (76 cm by 91.5cm)
London £30,800 ($39,424). 14.XI.84

*Opposite, above*
**Dame Laura Knight, DBE, RA**
WIND AND SUN
Watercolour and gouache over pencil on linen, signed, inscribed with the title on labels on
the backboard, *circa* 1911, 38in by 44⅛in (96.5cm by 112cm)
London £66,000 ($84,480). 15.V.85

*Opposite, below*
**Sir Alfred Munnings, PRA**
LAURA KNIGHT PAINTING
Signed, *circa* 1908, 20in by 24in (51cm by 61cm)
London £30,800 ($39,424). 15.V.85

**Jean-Baptiste-Camille Corot**
ROME: THE ISLAND AND BRIDGE OF SAN BARTOLOMEO
Oil on paper laid down on canvas, signed, *circa* 1826–28, 10¾in by 16⅞in (27.3cm by 42.9cm)
New York $935,000 (£730,469). 24.IV.85
From the collection of the late Florence J. Gould

*Opposite*
**Franz Xavier Winterhalter**
PORTRAIT OF CLAIRE DE BEARN, DUCHESS OF VALLOMBROSA
Signed and dated *Paris 1840*, 51¾in by 38¾in (131.5cm by 98.5cm)
New York $66,000 (£51,563). 23.V.85
From the collection of Mrs Charles Wrightsman

**Mary Ellen Best**

INTERIOR OF THE GREAT ROOM AT THE HOTEL DU CHEVAL D'OR, FRANKFURT
A/M, OPEN FOR THE EXHIBITION OF PICTURES, MAY 1835
Pencil and watercolour, signed and dated *May 1835*, and titled on the reverse,
12¾in by 16⅛in (32.5cm by 41cm)
New York $19,250 (£15,039). 19.X.84
From the collection of Ronald Graney and Thomas Sarg Graney

This watercolour is from an album of drawings made in 1835 by Mary Ellen Best, a gifted amateur from Yorkshire, on the first of three trips she made to Germany before her marriage in 1840.

*Opposite, above*
**Ludwig Koch**

THE POLO GAME
Watercolour and bodycolour over pencil, on paper laid down on canvas, signed and dated *1911*,
34⅞in by 58⅝in (88.5cm by 149cm)
London £28,600 ($36,608). 20.VI.85

**Aureliano de Beruete y Moret**
THE BANKS OF THE EGA
Signed, *circa* 1886, 39⅝in by 70in (100.5cm by 178cm)
Madrid Ptas 8,280,000 (£37,130 : $47,586). 27.II.85

**William-Adolphe Bouguereau**
LOVE DISARMED
Signed and dated *1885*, 47¼in by 38¼in (120cm by 97cm)
New York $126,500 (£98,828). 23.V.85

**Ernst Klimt and Gustav Klimt**
A THEATRICAL BUFFOON ON A MAKESHIFT STAGE IN ROTHENBURG OB DER TAUBER
Signed by Ernst Klimt, 58½in by 69in (148.6cm by 175.4cm)
London £154,000 ($197,120). 27.XI.84

Before coming to prominence as one of the leaders of the Vienna Secession movement, Gustav Klimt
was a successful establishment artist. This painting, the original version of which was commissioned
for the Burgtheater in Vienna in 1881, was finished by Gustav after the death in 1892 of his brother
Ernst, whose signature Gustav probably added. The Klimts' sisters and Emilie Flöge, Gustav's
lifelong companion, acted as models.

**Jean Béraud**
ON THE BOULEVARD AT THE CAFE TORTONI
Signed, 25in by 32in (63.5cm by 81.2cm)
New York $203,500 (£158,984). 23.V.85

*Opposite*
**Lovis Corinth**
PORTRAIT OF ELLY
Signed twice and inscribed *Elly*, 1889, 74⅜in by 43½in (189cm by 110.5cm)
London £99,000 ($126,720). 18.VI.85

# The Coral Petroleum Collection
# of Orientalist paintings:
# a twentieth-century response to
# a nineteenth-century enthusiasm

MaryAnne Stevens

To a nineteenth-century collector, Orientalist pictures would have been seen as one aspect of contemporary European painting. In the greatest collections, pictures of archaeological sites, the desert and the Nile, harems and odalisques hung comfortably beside scenes of European life. A collection, such as the one assembled by Coral Petroleum, Inc., devoted exclusively to Orientalist works, represents a comparatively recent departure and presents an opportunity to study the phenomenon of Orientalism in the nineteenth century, both in cultural and in art historical terms.

There appear to have been four guiding impulses behind the nineteenth-century enthusiasm for the Near East. In line with shifting perceptions of the nude was an apparent and prurient desire to enjoy the forbidden pleasures of the odalisque, albeit in surrogate form. Secondly, there was a genuine interest in the mysterious world of Islam, revealed by some European artists of the Romantic tradition, such as Delacroix and Renoir, through dazzling colour and light, while others, trained in the Realist school, concentrated upon a scrupulous rendition of characteristic landscapes, local *mores* and specific ethnographic types, as seen in the work of Eugène-Alexis Girardet, Eugène Fromentin or Gustave-Achille Guillaumet. Seen as accurate depictions of the landscape and peoples of the Bible, such paintings were of interest to scholars and devout Christians of all persuasions and reveal another aspect of Orientalism: a fascination with what was deemed by some to be the purity and spiritual superiority of the Islamic faith. Finally, and most significantly, there was a market created by a growing number of Europeans whose political and cultural interests were engaged in the Near East and North Africa, among them the great collector Sir Richard Wallace and the Duc d'Aumâle, leader of the French forces in North Africa, who added Orientalist paintings to their collections as souvenirs of their experiences.

The Coral Collection highlighted two themes peculiar to nineteenth-century Orientalism: the harem and the Islamic world. The exoticism of the harem subject, as well as its obvious sexual implications, captivated the imagination. Crystalised in the

Fig. 1
**John Frederick Lewis, RA**
AN INTERCEPTED CORRESPONDENCE
On panel, signed and dated *1869*, 29¼in by 34⅜in (74.3cm by 87.3cm)
New York $1,265,000 (£988,281). 22.V.85
From the collection of Coral Petroleum, Inc.

The scene shows a woman of the harem caught with a bouquet from an illicit lover. Contemporary accounts relate that flowers were customarily used as love letters, each flower having a particular significance. In 1869, the year that Lewis painted this picture, *The Young Ladies' Journal* published *The Language of Flowers* in which the preface stated that this form of communication originated in the Middle East and the glossary went on to interpret the symbolic meaning of various flowers.

Fig. 3
**Jean Léon Gérôme**
THE WHIRLING DERVISHES
Signed, *circa* 1895, 28½in by 37in (72.5cm by 94cm)
New York $352,000 (£275,000). 22.V.85
From the collection of Coral Petroleum, Inc.

*Opposite*
Fig. 2
**Ludwig Deutsch**
THE NUBIAN GUARD
On panel, signed and dated *Paris 1902*, 25¾in by 18¼in (65.5cm by 46.4cm)
New York $159,500 (£124,609). 22.V.85
From the collection of Coral Petroleum, Inc.

work of Jean-Auguste-Dominique Ingres, who travelled no further south or east than Rome, the genre had emerged during the eighteenth century in the 'turqueries' of Van Loo. Drawing upon historical sources such as the letters of Lady Mary Wortley Montagu and Montesquieu's *Lettres persanes*, and upon engravings culled from old travel books, Ingres depicted a hothouse world in which he created a compromise between Eastern and Western standards of beauty, drawing the spectator into a world of forbidden sexual pleasures. For many travellers this was the most alluring attraction of their journey, and the source of innumerable literary and pictorial representations, including Gérard de Nerval's imaginary longings: 'Does one not dream of adventure and mysteries at the sight of these tall houses, these latticed windows, where so often one sees the sparkle of the inquiring eyes of young girls.'

It is within this context that the *Intercepted correspondence* by J.F. Lewis (Fig. 1) should be viewed. It would appear from the scant information available that Lewis almost certainly enjoyed a modest harem during his ten-year sojourn in Cairo (1840–50). European women were able to enter the harems and commented upon them with respect and admiration, but few European men ever gained access to the women's quarters, although Delacroix was a notable exception. He visited a harem in Algiers and used the experience as the source for his celebrated *Women of Algiers* of 1834 (Louvre, Paris). In the Coral Collection it is the hint of erotic experience found in works such as Ludwig Deutsch's *Nubian guard* (Fig. 2) or Gérôme's *Harem in the kiosk* that established the reality behind the popular illusion. Set against the backdrop of the walls of Constantinople, the women in Gérôme's painting are physically and symbolically separated from the spectator by their heavy veils, the half shadow of the kiosk, the stone parapet and the armed guard in the foreground.

For many devout Christians, Islam was a heresy, the various manifestations of which, as seen in the howling and whirling dervishes painted by Gérôme (Fig. 3) and Albert Aublet, provided conclusive evidence of its inherently barbaric nature. But there was another, equally potent vision of Islam. For Paul Lenoir, who accompanied Gérôme on his journey to the Near East in 1868, the observation of Muslims at prayer served to highlight the impoverished state of European Christianity: 'The thing that strikes you most when you visit mosques is their exclusively religious, almost poetic, atmosphere. These are not our pretty-pretty Parisian cathedrals, nor our phoney-Greek temples, which are just theatres where the performance is the Mass. Seeing quiet, serious Arabs prostrate themselves without affectation before the wall of miḥrab, I could not help thinking of my good old Madeleine, where the one-o'clock service is just like the opening night of a show . . . In Cairo, it is fanaticism if you like, but at least it is real religious faith . . . without any of that elegant, frivolous piety that characterises the Roman Catholic mosque back home.' Gérôme's *Prayers in the Quayt-Bey mosque, Cairo* and the *Muezzin's call to prayer* (Fig. 4), capture Lenoir's sense of awe, recording the reality of Allah in the Muslim world.

Orientalist paintings may tell us more about the aesthetic preoccupations of the West than of the reality of life in the Near East and North Africa. But, hung upon the walls of exhibition halls and in the private apartments of connoisseurs, they testify to the fascination that the Near East has held for painters and collectors alike.

Fig. 4
**Jean Léon Gérôme**
THE MUEZZIN'S CALL TO PRAYER
Signed, *circa* 1879–80, 35½in by 25¾in (90.2cm by 65.4cm)
New York $440,000 (£343,750). 22.V.85
From the collection of Coral Petroleum, Inc.

**Rudolf von Alt**
FIGURES ON A BRIDGE OVER A STREAM AT GASTEIN
Watercolour and bodycolour, signed and dated *Gastein '88*,
19⅞in by 13¼in (50.5cm by 33.5cm)
London £26,400 ($33,792). 20.VI.85

**Giovanni Segantini**
A COW AT A WATER TROUGH
Signed and dated *1892*, 20⅛in by13⅜in (51cm by 34cm)
Zürich SFr 638,000 (£192,749:$246,332). 13.VI.85

**Peder Severin Krøyer**
FISHERMEN ON THE BEACH AT SKAGEN
Signed and dated *Skagen 1891*, 48⅜in by 88¾in (123cm by 225.5cm)
London £242,000 ($309,760). 18.VI.85

**Anders Zorn**
SELF-PORTRAIT
Signed, *circa* 1889, 28in by 23⅜in (71cm by 59.5cm)
London £115,500 ($147,840). 18.VI.85

**Claude Monet**
IN THE GARDEN: THE ARTIST'S FAMILY
Signed, 1875, 24in by 31½in (61cm by 80cm)
New York $2,420,000 (£1,890,625). 14.XI.84
From the collection of Mr and Mrs David Bakalar

This painting shows the artist's wife Camille, his son Jean and their maid in the garden of their house at Argenteuil.

**Gustave Caillebotte**
THE BASSIN D'ARGENTEUIL
*Circa* 1882, 25¾in by 31⅞in (65.5cm by 81cm)
New York $473,000 (£369,531). 14.V.85

# The Gould Collection
# of Impressionist paintings

John L. Tancock

With exhibitions in Tokyo, London, Lausanne, an extended pre-sale exhibition in New York and preceded by press coverage that at times seemed to rival that of an American presidential campaign, the sale of Impressionist paintings and drawings from the estate of Florence J. Gould took place on 24 April 1985 in New York. There was always the risk that the evening might turn out to be something of an anticlimax, but happily this was not the case.

Mrs Gould began collecting paintings seriously after the death of her husband Frank J. Gould in 1955, but it should be stressed that her aim never was to form a collection that made a systematic survey of French painting of the nineteenth century and the modern era. Rather, the collection should be seen as one aspect of her desire to create not only for herself but for her many friends, an ambience of the greatest refinement and luxury, enhanced by a splendid array of paintings and drawings, furniture and works of art. Many are the accounts of her lavish lunches and soirées, and none more perceptive than that of Peter Wilson in the foreword to the catalogues of the sales of Mrs Gould's collection. While never having set out to obtain an unrivalled assembly of masterpieces, Florence Gould's collection contained a certain number of works from the nineteenth and twentieth centuries that rank highly in any account of French painting, as well as many more that are quintessential statements of the suavity and charm of the style of painting that first emerged in France in the eighteenth century, with the work of Watteau, and later of Boucher.

Florence Gould spent the greater part of her life in the south of France, living first at a villa called La Vigie at Juan les Pins and, from 1955 onwards, at El Patio outside Cannes. With one outstanding exception, Camille Pissarro's *Rue de la Citadelle, Pontoise* (Fig. 1), seen in the light of an overcast snowy day, her pictures are characterised by the brilliant light of the south, as depicted by Van Gogh (Fig. 2) and Cézanne. In Corot's *Rome: the island and bridge of San Bartolomeo, circa* 1826–28, painted during the first of his three trips to Italy, the crystalline light defines the architectural forms with the utmost clarity, resulting in an image of classical but not cold perfection. For many, the artist's *View of the Pincio, Italy* was no less desirable, although it sold for the relatively modest sum of $220,000.

Fig. 1
**Camille Pissarro**
RUE DE LE CITADELLE, PONTOISE
Signed and dated *1873*, 21¼in by 29in (54cm by 73.7cm)
New York $935,000 (£730,469). 24.IV.85
From the collection of the late Florence J. Gould

Cézanne painted this same scene from a slightly different perspective when he was living at Pontoise to be near Pissarro. The two artists worked closely together at this period, frequently setting up their easels next to each other, but usually facing in different directions, making it difficult to identify works painted contemporaneously.

Fig. 2
**Vincent Van Gogh**
LANDSCAPE WITH THE RISING SUN
November 1889, 28¾in by 36¼in (73cm by 92cm)
New York $9,900,000 (£7,734,375). 24.IV.85
From the collection of the late Florence J. Gould

Van Gogh was admitted to the asylum at St Rémy as a
voluntary patient on 8 May 1889, where the view from
his room provided his principal experience of the outside
world. On 25 May he wrote to his brother Theo:
'Through the iron-barred window I see a square field of
wheat in an enclosure, a perspective like van Goyen,
above which I see the morning sun rising in all its glory.'

The anxiety-plagued young Cézanne was as different in personality as could be from the Corot who painted the Roman pictures. When he painted *Chestnut trees and farm at the Jas de Bouffan*, a view of the family estate outside Aix-en-Provence, the beneficial influence of Pissarro enabled Cézanne to focus on an attempt to extract such order as he perceived in the ever-changing aspects of the landscape and light of the south. Monet found dealing with the dazzling southern light a perpetual struggle, although there is no sign of this in the brilliant shimmer of the most seductive of pictures, *Antibes seen from the Jardins de la Salis* (Fig. 3), painted in 1888.

Van Gogh's *Landscape with the rising sun* (Fig. 2) was painted the following year when the artist was a patient at the hospital of St Paul at St Rémy and, while the price was remarkable, the picture was even more so. The motif, a field seen from the upper storey of the asylum, the enclosing wall and low hills beyond, was scarcely distinguished, but as described in Vincent's letters to his brother Theo, it gains a powerful resonance and in its realisation confirms Van Gogh as one of the greatest of pictorial intelligences.

Although Mrs Gould lived in a part of the world where flowers are abundant, she liked to be surrounded by flower paintings. Her collection contained two superb floral still lifes by Fantin-Latour and a monumental example by Courbet, *Bouquet of flowers in a vase* (Fig. 4). Never one for half measures, either in his life or in his painting, Courbet filled his vase with a dazzling array of flowers, which becomes a wonderful depiction of the amplitude of nature on canvas.

Landscapes, flowers and portraits all captivated Florence Gould. Berthe Morisot's *Behind the Venetian blind (Resting)*, shows the artist, in spite of her affiliation with the Impressionists, to have been in direct line of descent from the great decorative painters of the eighteenth century in the sensibility of the young girl. Renoir's *Girl in a straw hat*, a study for *The outing to the Conservatoire* in the Barnes Foundation, probably depicts Angèle, a Montmartre flower-seller who, in her freshness and apparent innocence, contrasts markedly with Toulouse-Lautrec's *Clowness Cha-u-Kao* (Fig. 5). Cha-u-Kao was a dancer at the Moulin Rouge and the Nouveau Cirque whose notorious life-style and picturesque costumes appealed to Toulouse-Lautrec on many levels. In this work, unlike other portraits of her in the Musée d'Orsay, the Musée du Jeu de Paume and the Oskar Reinhart Collection (Winterthur), the background is only partially sketched in, but this places all the emphasis on the dancer herself, who appears lost in thought. Much less ambitious although no less penetrating, Toulouse-Lautrec's *At the 'Star' Le Havre (Miss Dolly, the English singer)* depicts an entertainer he encountered while passing through Le Havre on the way to Bordeaux in 1899.

With the gradual dispersal of Florence Gould's various collections, culminating in the sale of paintings in New York in April, the disappearance of a flamboyant way of life was sadly marked, but Mrs Gould's devotion to the life and culture of France will be perpetuated through the Florence J. Gould Foundation, the principal purpose of which is the furthering of Franco-American amity.

Fig. 3
**Claude Monet**
ANTIBES SEEN FROM THE JARDINS DE LA SALIS
Signed and dated *88*, 25⅝in by 36¼in (65cm by 92cm)
New York $1,375,000 (£1,074,219). 24.IV.85
From the collection of the late Florence J. Gould

Monet arrived in Antibes on 14 January 1888. On 14 June Theo Van Gogh purchased ten Antibes paintings from the artist for FF11,900 and, agreeing to split the anticipated profit, exhibited them in Paris to great critical acclaim.

Fig. 4
**Gustave Courbet**
BOUQUET OF FLOWERS IN A VASE
Signed and dated *62*, 39½in by 28¾in (100.3cm by 73cm)
New York $1,210,000 (£945,313). 24.IV.85
From the collection of the late Florence J. Gould

Fig. 5
**Henri de Toulouse-Lautrec**
THE CLOWNESS CHA-U-KAO
On board, signed, 1895, $31\frac{7}{8}$in by $23\frac{1}{2}$in (81cm by 59.7cm)
New York $5,280,000 (£4,125,000). 24.IV.85
From the collection of the late Florence J. Gould

**Claude Monet**
THE JAPANESE BRIDGE IN MONET'S GARDEN
Painted *circa* 1895–96 but signed and dated later *1900*, 35in by 36¼in (89cm by 92cm)
London £1,056,000 ($1,351,680). 4.XII.84

*Opposite*
**Pierre-Auguste Renoir**
STANDING BATHER
Signed and dated *96*, 31⅞in by 24in (81cm by 61cm)
New York $1,980,000 (£1,546,875). 14.V.85

**Gustave Caillebotte**
WOMAN AT HER TOILETTE
Stamped with signature, *circa* 1873, 25⅝in by 31⅞in (65cm by 81cm)
New York $605,000 (£472,656). 16.XI.84
From the collection of the late Pauline K. Cave

**Edouard Vuillard**
BREAKFAST
On board, signed with initials and dated *93*, 12⅛in by 10½in (30.7cm by 26.6cm)
New York $187,000 (£146,094). 15.XI.84
From the collection of the late Emily Milliken Wilson

**Wassily Kandinsky**
THE ELEPHANT
On board, signed, 1908, 18⅛in by 27in (46cm by 68.5cm)
London £462,000 ($591,360). 4.XII.84

**André Derain**
TREES ON A RIVER BANK
Signed and dated *1905*, 23⅝in by 31⅞in (60cm by 81cm)
London £671,000 ($858,880). 4.XII.84

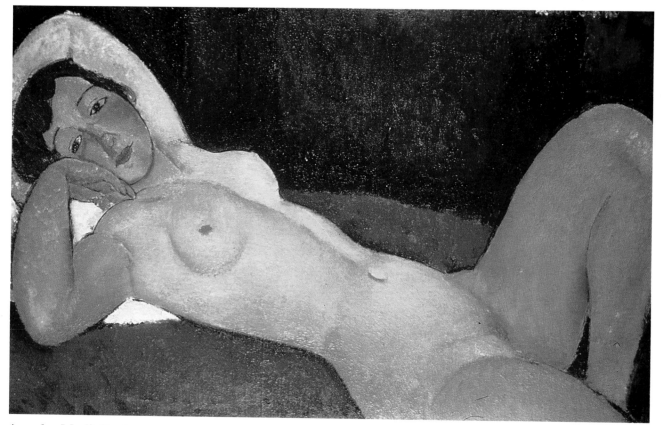

**Amedeo Modigliani**
THE DREAMER
Signed, *circa* 1917–18, 23½in by 36¼in (59.7cm by 92cm)
New York $4,620,000 (£3,609,375). 14.XI.84

*Opposite*
**Pablo Picasso**
LA GOMMEUSE
Signed, 1901, 31⅞in by 21¼in (81cm by 54cm)
London £1,430,000 ($1,830,400). 4.XII.84

**Egon Schiele**
SUMMER LANDSCAPE, KRUMAU
Signed and dated *1917*, 43½in by 54¾in (110.5cm by 139cm)
New York $2,530,000 (£1,976,563). 14.V.85

*Opposite*
**Giorgio de Chirico**
THE DEPARTURE OF THE POET
Signed, 1914, 33⅞in by 25⅞in (86cm by 65.7cm)
New York $1,045,000 (£816,406). 14.XI.84

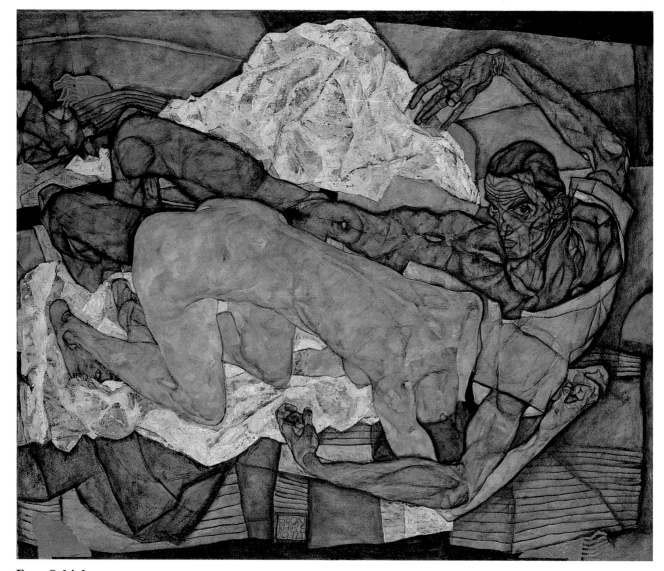

**Egon Schiele**
LOVERS: MAN AND WOMAN I
Signed and dated *1914*, 46$\frac{7}{8}$in by 54$\frac{3}{4}$in (119cm by 139cm)
London £3,190,000 ($4,083,200). 4.XII.84

**Egon Schiele**
TWO SEATED GIRLS
Watercolour over pencil heightened with white gouache, signed and dated *1911*,
17¼in by 12in (43.7cm by 30.3cm)
London £192,500 ($246,400). 26.VI.85

**Léon Bakst**
COSTUME DESIGN FOR IDA RUBINSTEIN AS ST SEBASTIAN IN 'LE MARTYRE DE
ST SEBASTIEN'
Sanguine, signed and dated *1911*, 27⅜in by 16in (69.5cm by 40.5cm)
London £29,700 ($38,016). 28.V.85

**Pablo Picasso**
DESIGN FOR THE DECOR OF 'LE TRICORNE'
Watercolour, signed and dated *Londres 1919*, 7¾in by 10¼in (19.7cm by 26cm)
New York $37,400 (£29,219). 21.XI.84

**Fernand Léger**
STUDY FOR 'THE TUG BOAT'
Pen and brush and ink and watercolour, signed with initials and dated '18,
9⅝in by 13⅛in (24.5cm by 33.5cm)
London £107,800 ($137,984). 26.VI.85

**Henri Matisse**
LE SILENCE HABITE DES MAISONS
Brush and indian ink on paper, signed and dated *juin 47*, 24¼in by 19¼in (61.5cm by 49cm)
New York $176,000 (£137,500). 15.V.85

**Alberto Giacometti**
DIEGO IN AN INTERIOR
Signed and dated *1949–50*, 29⅛in by 17⅛in (74cm by 43.5cm)
London £253,000 ($323,840). 4.XII.84

**Pablo Picasso**
THE MISTLETOE SELLER
Gouache, signed, 1902–1903, 21¼in by 15in (54cm by 38cm)
New York $1,100,000 (£859,375). 14.V.85

**Henri Rousseau called Le Douanier**
THE PROMENADE AT BUTTES-CHAUMONT
Signed, *circa* 1908, 18⅛in by 15in (46cm by 38cm)
London £187,000 ($239,360). 26.III.85

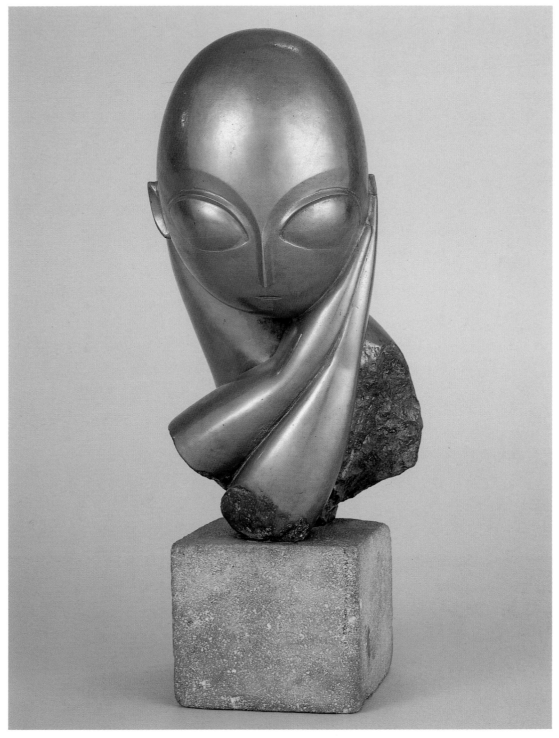

**Constantin Brancusi**

MLLE POGANY

Bronze, signed, stamped with the foundry mark *C. Valsuani cire perdue*, 1913, height 17½in (44.5cm)
New York $1,650,000 (£1,289,063). 14.XI.84

Margit Pogany, a Hungarian artist living in Paris, posed for this sculpture in 1910 and 1911.

**René Magritte**
LA CORDE SENSIBLE
Signed, and signed, titled and dated *1960* on the reverse, 44⅛in by 57⅛in (112cm by 145cm)
London £352,000 ($450,560). 4.XII.84

*Opposite*
**Max Ernst**
CAPRICORN
Bronze, signed and numbered *o/v*, 1964, height 98⅜in (250cm)
New York $962,500 (£751,953). 14.V.85
From the collection of Joel Mallin

In 1946 Max Ernst and Dorothea Tanning moved to Arizona where *Capricorn* was conceived in 1948.
The monumental group, which was eventually cast in 1964, is considered to be an encyclopaedia of
Ernst's sculptural motifs.

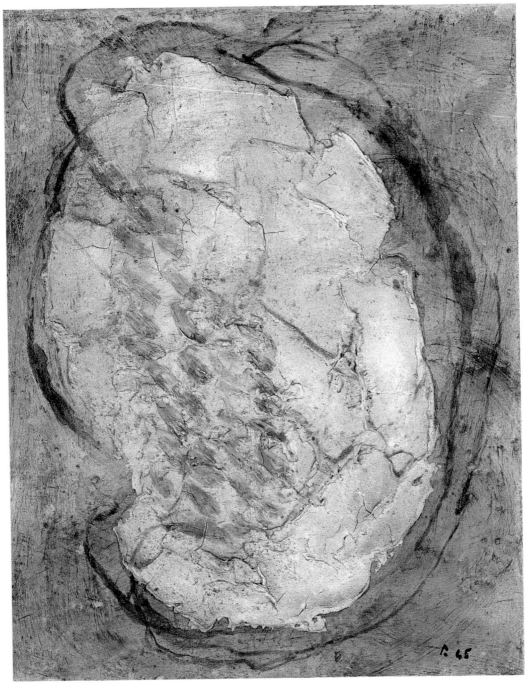

**Jean Fautrier**
TETE D'OTAGE NO 24
Signed with initial and dated '45, 13¾in by 10⅝in (35cm by 27cm)
London £126,500 ($161,920). 6.XII.84

This work was executed *circa* 1942–44, although like the majority of the *Otage* series, which Fautrier painted while in hiding from the Germans, it was not signed and dated until the end of the war.

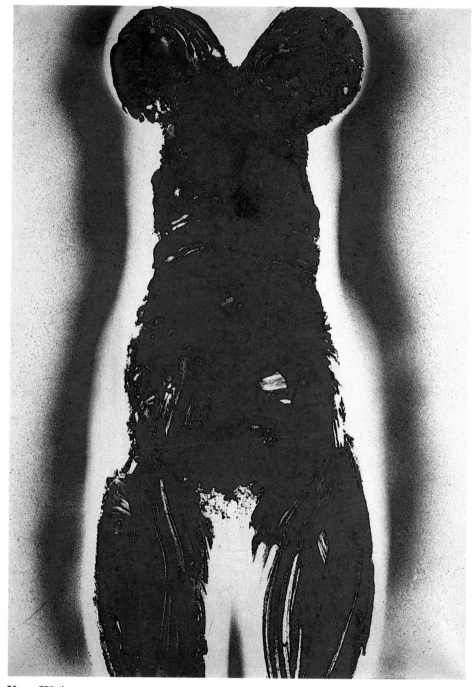

**Yves Klein**
ANTHROMETRIE 11
Pigment on paper, 1960, 29⅞in by 20⅞in (76cm by 53cm)
London £37,400 ($47,872). 27.VI.85

**Willem de Kooning**
RUTH'S ZOWIE
1957, 80¼in by 70⅛in (204cm by 178cm)
New York $1,540,000 (£1,203,125). 2.V.85
From the collection of the late Thomas B. Hess

**Francis Bacon**
LANDSCAPE NEAR MALABATA, TANGIERS
Titled and dated *1963* on the reverse, 76½in by 56in (194.5cm by 142.2cm)
New York $517,000 (£403,906). 2.V.85
From the collection of Miss Patricia Neal

**Barnett Newman**
ULYSSES
Signed and dated *1952*, 132in by 50in (335.5cm by 127cm)
New York $1,595,000 (£1,246,094). 2.V.85
From the collection of Christophe de Menil

**Roy Lichtenstein**
RECLINING NUDE
Oil and magna on canvas, signed and dated '77 on the reverse, 84in by 120in (213.4cm by 304.8cm)
New York $522,500 (£408,203). 2.V.85

**Clyfford Still**
UNTITLED
Signed and dated *1954–NYC* twice on the reverse, 117in by 93in (297.2cm by 236.3cm)
New York $797,500 (£623,047). 2.V.85
From the collection of François de Menil

**Mark Rothko**
UNTITLED
1960, 93in by 81in (236.3cm by 205.7cm)
New York $715,000 (£558,594). 2.V.85

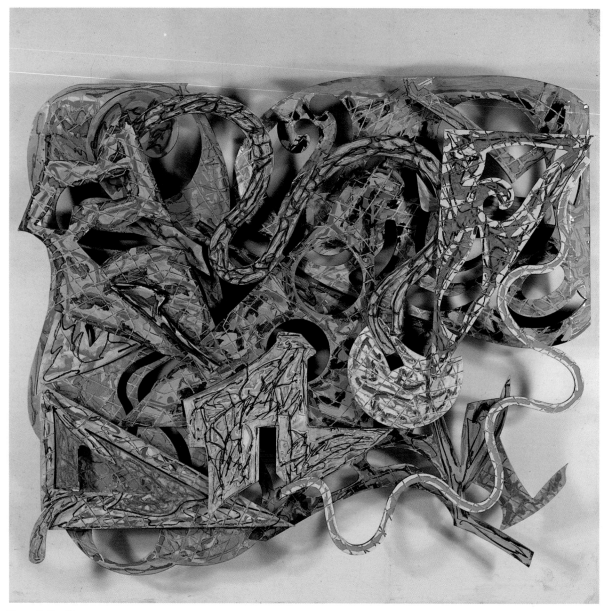

**Frank Stella**
ANDERSTORP
Mixed media on etched magnesium, 1981, 108¼in by 123½in by 15¾in (275cm by 314cm by 40cm)
New York $319,000 (£249,219). 31.X.84

**David Hockney**
PLAY WITHIN A PLAY
Oil on canvas with painted plexiglass overlay, 1963, 78in by 84in (198.2cm by 213.4cm)
New York $253,000 (£197,656). 31.X.84

### Thomas Birch

THE BATTERY AND HARBOR, NEW YORK
Inscribed *Tho' B(ir)ch New York, circa* 1810–11, 29in by 41in (73.7cm by 104.2cm)
New York $181,500 (£141,797). 6.XII.84

Birch's painting can be dated by the inclusion on the left of Castle Williams, which was completed on 10 January 1810.

**Martin Johnson Heade**
HUMMING BIRDS
Signed, 20in by 12in
(50.8cm by 30.5cm)
New York $192,500 (£150,391)
6.XII.84

**William Merritt Chase**
ON THE LAKE, CENTRAL PARK
On panel, signed, titled on a label on the reverse, *circa* 1894, 14in by 16in (35.5cm by 40.6cm)
New York $473,000 (£369,531). 30.V.85

**Theodore Robinson**
THE WATERING POTS
Signed, and signed, titled and inscribed *11 E.14th St.* on a label on the stretcher, 1890,
18in by 22in (45.7cm by 55.9cm)
New York $258,500 (£201,953). 30.V.85

This is one of a series of pictures Robinson painted in June 1890 at Giverny.

**Sanford Robinson Gifford**
NOMAN'S LAND
Signed and dated *1877*, and signed, dated and titled on the reverse, 9¼in by 16¼in (23.5cm by 41.3cm)
New York $203,500 (£158,984). 6.XII.84

**Frederic Remington**
AN ASSAULT ON HIS DIGNITY
Signed and dated *Copyright 1906*, 27in by 40in (68.6cm by 101.6cm)
New York $627,000 (£489,844). 30.V.85
From the collection of the late Gwendolyn S. Anderson

*Opposite*
**Thomas Moran**
ZION VALLEY, SOUTH UTAH
Signed with monogram and thumb print and dated *1916*, and titled on a label on the stretcher,
22in by 42¼in (55.9cm by 107.3cm)
New York $308,000 (£240,625). 30.V.85

**Willard Leroy Metcalf**
THE LANDING PLACE
Signed and dated '04, 26in by 29in (66cm by 73.7cm)
New York $148,500 (£116,016). 6.XII.84

**Winslow Homer**

INLAND WATER, BERMUDA

Watercolour, signed and dated *1901*, and titled on the reverse, 13¾in by 21in (34.9cm by 53.3cm)

New York $319,000 (£249,219). 6.XII.84

From the collection of the Fine Arts Committee of the United States Department of State

**John Singer Sargent**
VENICE, PALAZZO LABIA
Signed and dated *1913*, 22in by 28in (55.9cm by 71.2cm)
New York $363,000 (£283,594). 6.XII.84
From the Ormond Collection

Sargent said of this evening scene that it was the closest he had ever got to those effects he wished to realise in landscape.

**Richard Emil Miller**
CAFE DE LA PAIX
Signed, *circa* 1905, 45in by 57¾in (114.3cm by 146.7cm)
New York $275,000 (£214,844). 30.V.85

**Grant Wood**

ARBOR DAY

On panel, signed and dated *1932*, 25in by 30in (63.5cm by 76.2cm)

New York $1,375,000 (£1,074,219). 30.V.85

This painting, commissioned by Cedar Rapids school, Iowa, shows a schoolmistress and her pupils planting a tree to provide shade for the schoolhouse. Wood chose not to paint the contemporary schoolhouse of the 1930s, surrounded by full-grown trees, but as it might have looked in the 1890s, when the custom of planting a tree each year was first introduced.

**Charles E. Burchfield**
OCTOBER IN THE WOODS
Watercolour, signed with monogram and dated *1938–63*, 45in by 57in (114.3cm by 144.8cm)
New York $148,500 (£116,016). 6.XII.84
From the Altman Collection

**Adam Willaerts**
THE MAN-O'-WAR 'AMSTERDAM' AND OTHER DUTCH SHIPS IN TABLE BAY
Signed, *circa* 1636, 36⅝in by 52in (93cm by 132cm)
Johannesburg R190,000 (£74,219:$95,477). 6.XI.84

This is the earliest recorded painting of the Cape and probably depicts the landing of the Dutch fleet under the command of Hendrik Brouwer on 9 March 1636.

*Opposite*
**Eugen von Guérard**
SYDNEY HEADS
Signed and dated *1860*, 19⅛in by 30in (48.5cm by 76.3cm)
Sydney Aus $200,000 (£103,627:$132,450). 17.X.84
From the collection of the late G. K. Cowlishaw

**Samuel Thomas Gill**

CITY OF SYDNEY FROM NORTH SHORE

Watercolour, signed and dated '56, $13\frac{1}{2}$in by $23\frac{3}{8}$in (34.2cm by 59.4cm)

Sydney Aus $75,000 (£38,860:$49,669). 17.X.84

From the collection of the late G. K. Cowlishaw

**Frida Kahlo**
THE LITTLE DEER
On masonite, signed, inscribed and dated '*46*, 8¾in by 11¾in (22.2cm by 29.9cm)
New York $154,000 (£120,313). 28.V.85

The head of the wounded deer is a self portrait. Many of Frida Kahlo's works show a concern with suffering that can be traced to the physical injuries she received in a road accident in 1925, and to the emotional problems she experienced during the years of the breakdown of her marriage and eventual divorce from Diego Rivera in the '30s and early '40s.

*Opposite*
**Diego Rivera**
WOMEN WASHING CLOTHES IN A RIVER AMONG ZOPILOTES
Signed and dated '*28*, 33⅜in by 25½in (84.7cm by 64.8cm)
New York $170,500 (£133,203). 27.XI.84
From the collection of Evaline M. Foley

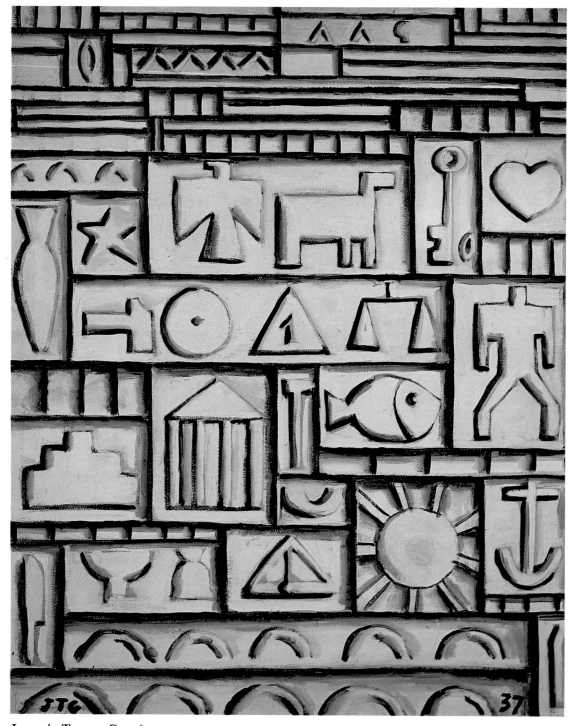

**Joaquin Torres-García**
CONSTRUCTIVIST RELIEF IN BLACK AND WHITE
Tempera on board, signed with initials and dated '37, 39⅝in by 31⅞in (100.7cm by 81cm)
New York $99,000 (£77,344). 28.V.85

**Rufino Tamayo**
NIÑA BONITA
Signed and dated '*37*, 48in by 36½in (122cm by 91.7cm)
New York $176,000 (£137,500). 28.V.85
From the collection of Mrs Edmund D. Smith

# The mature works of Wifredo Lam

Edward J. Sullivan

In September 1984 the Museum of Modern Art hung Wifredo Lam's *The jungle* as part of its exhibition of '"Primitivism" in 20th-Century Art'. Although this work had been on view in the museum for many years, attracting the attention of artists from the abstract to the Neo-Expressionist schools, it had always been exhibited among other examples of European and American modernism, never, until then, alongside the masks, hangings, constructions and works of art of African, Asian and American tribes. The inclusion of Lam's masterpiece in the exhibition underlined the importance of his art, derived from a myriad of both new and old world sources, and his position among the international modernists, whose work was profoundly influenced by tribal art.

Lam was born in Sagua la Grande, Cuba, in 1902. His father was a Chinese merchant, his mother of Afro-European descent. His godmother, Mantonica Wilson, was a practitioner of the occult arts, brought to Cuba from Africa by slaves in the eighteenth and nineteenth centuries. Michel de Leiris suggests, in his monograph on the artist (1970), that her influence on the young Lam was of prime importance. Many elements from Lam's Afro-Caribbean heritage are incorporated into his art, which presents as intense a blend of creative forces as can be found in the work of any contemporary artist.

After an early artistic training in Cuba, Wifredo Lam went to Spain in 1923, settling in Madrid where he studied at the Prado and worked in the studio of the academic painter Sotomayor, who was also a director of the museum. Lam was particularly fascinated by the bizarre imagery in the works of Bosch and Brueghel the Elder, according to his biographer Max-Pol Fouchet. He was also introduced to African art at this time, a passion that remained with him for the rest of his career. In 1937, during the Spanish Civil War, Lam left Madrid for Paris where he met Picasso. The impact of this meeting was enormous and much of Lam's work during the remainder of the 1930s is derived directly from Picasso's earlier renditions of the human figure of 1907–1908. At this period Lam also met members of the Surrealist circle, including André Breton, with whom he formed a particular friendship and for whom he illustrated the 'Fata Morgana'.

In 1941 Lam embarked with Breton and other French intellectuals for Cuba where, during the war years, he developed his intensely personal and unmistakable

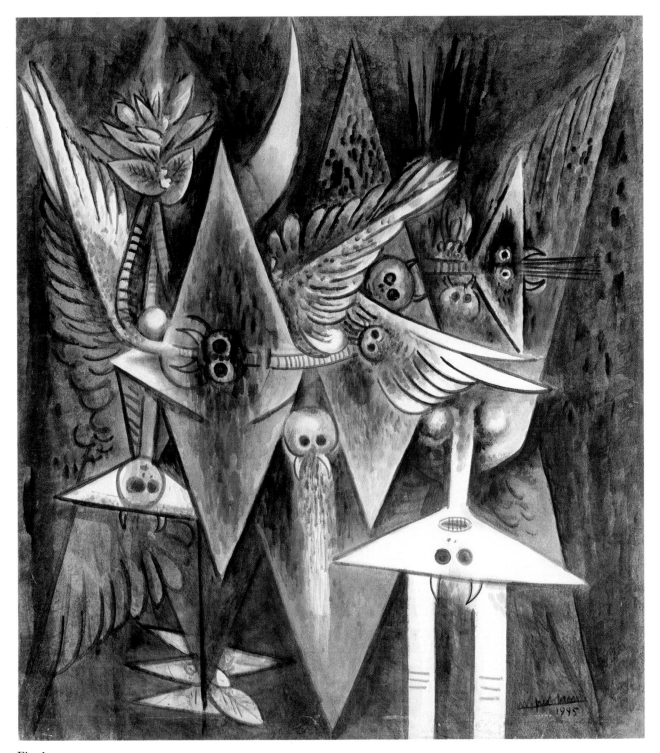

Fig. 1
**Wifredo Lam**
THE CARIBBEAN PARADE
Signed and dated *1945*, 49in by 43in (124.5cm by 109.2cm)
New York $214,500 (£167,578). 27.XI.84
From the collection of the late Joseph Cantor

Fig. 3
**Wifredo Lam**
CARIBBEAN ROOSTER
On jute, signed and dated *1954*, 28¼in by 35½in (71.8cm by 90.2cm)
New York $44,000 (£34,375). 27.XI.84
From the collection of the late Joseph Cantor

*Opposite*
Fig. 2
**Wifredo Lam**
THE OFFERING
Signed and dated *1950*, 52in by 40in (132cm by 101.5cm)
New York $110,000 (£85,938). 27.XI.84
From the collection of the late Joseph Cantor

iconography. He combined the inspiration of Picasso's work from the 1930s, especially *Guernica*, with the vibrant colours and rhythms of the Caribbean people and landscape. Although Lam did not by any means forsake traditional Western imagery, an often ecstatically mystical quality is infused into the works done after 1944, the year in which he and Breton went to Haiti, and where Lam was introduced to voodoo. In paintings like *Song of Osmosis* and *Caribbean parade* (Fig. 1), both 1945, the artist evokes an eerie world of the spirits of the jungle creatures, brought to the Caribbean by slaves. These canvases are characterised by numerous small creatures with spiky, abbreviated facial features, reminiscent of the African art Lam had seen in Spain and France and of the tribal objects of the voodoo and *santería* (Cuban Afro-Antillean religion) cults. Jewel-like colours, deep reds, yellows and blues, punctuate both paintings.

Scintillating rhythms describe the *Song of the forest* of 1946 where the murky interior of a tropical forest is evoked; the mysterious rites and incantations to Dhambala, the voodoo goddess of unity; to Erzulie, the divinity of love and to Azacca, the god of agriculture. More explicit references to religious practices are seen in *The offering* of 1950 (Fig. 2) where a horned figure with streaming hair clasps two bird-like creatures in its hands. Birds appear with great frequency in Lam's art: the cock is often portrayed as a symbolic reference to the god of war, Osun. Two works of the early 1950s bear the title *Caribbean rooster*, one of which is illustrated here (Fig. 3). They show the bird in a much-transformed state, with prickly spikes instead of a comb, holding a dagger in one hand. These images also contain strong elements of political symbolism.

Lam's representations of women usually have abbreviated features, transposed anatomy and are sometimes headless or faceless. Three pictures recently sold at Sotheby's bear these characteristics, derived in large part from Picasso's work of the 1930s. In *Horse woman* of 1950 (Fig. 4), a subject Lam painted more than once, he transforms the woman into a hybrid horse form. The vibrant orange and yellow *Overture to Eleggua* represents the Afro-Cuban goddess of destiny holding a receptacle with the head of Osun. But perhaps the most fascinating of the female forms is the *Water braids* from 1950 (*Art at Auction* 1983–84) in which male and female characteristics are combined in one figure. The title refers to the luxurious head of hair cascading down the back of the woman, reminiscent of Lam's drawings for Breton's 'Fata Morgana', as Suzanne Carrigues-Daniel points out in the catalogue of the sale of 29 May 1984.

Wifredo Lam's art represents an extreme refinement and sophistication of native forms and ideological concepts, which he employs in a highly intellectual fashion. This he has in common with other creators of modern Cuban art, the more seriously thoughtful literary art of masters like the poet Nicolás Guillén or the contemporary novelists Alejo Carpentier and Guillermo Cabrera Infante, who, like Lam, delve into the infra-structure of their complex country. Dealing with the mystery of Afro-Antillean traditions, while sensitive to the international vocabulary of Surrealism and other art forms, Lam and his colleagues created a uniquely Cuban, but still universal genre of art.

Fig. 4
**Wifredo Lam**
HORSE WOMAN
Signed and dated *1950*, 48½in by 42½in (123.3cm by 108cm)
New York $104,500 (£81,641). 27.XI.84
From the collection of a subsidiary of PepsiCo., Inc.

# Prints

**Rembrandt Harmensz. van Rijn**
ABRAHAM FRANCEN, APOTHECARY
Etching and drypoint on Japan paper, fourth state of ten, $6\frac{1}{4}$in by $8\frac{1}{8}$in (16cm by 20.7cm)
London £44,000 ($56,320). 27.VI.85

**Rembrandt Harmensz. van Rijn**
SHEET OF STUDIES: HEAD OF THE ARTIST,
A BEGGAR COUPLE, HEAD OF AN OLD MAN AND OF
AN OLD WOMAN
Etching, second state of two, *circa* 1632,
$3\frac{7}{8}$in by $4\frac{1}{8}$in (10cm by 10.5cm)
New York $29,700 (£23,203). 10.V.85

**James Barry**
EASTERN PATRIARCH
Pen-lithograph on laid paper, 1803,
$9\frac{1}{4}$in by $12\frac{3}{4}$in (23.4cm by 32.3cm)
London £5,940 ($7,603). 7.III.85

**Henri de Toulouse-Lautrec**

PARTIE DE CAMPAGNE

Lithograph printed in colours on wove paper, stamped with monogram, numbered *8*, published 1897,
15¾in by 20⅜in (40cm by 51.8cm)
New York $99,000 (£77,344). 9.V.85

This lithograph was the eighth of 100 original prints published by Vollard in *L'Album d'éstampes
originales de la Galerie Vollard*.

*Opposite*

**Mary Cassatt**

WOMAN BATHING or LA TOILETTE

Drypoint, soft ground etching and aquatint printed in colours on heavy laid paper, signed in pencil
and inscribed *à Monsieur Leroy*, *circa* 1891, proof aside from the edition of twenty-five,
sheet size 18⅝in by 12⅛in (47.3cm by 30.9cm)
New York $93,500 (£73,047). 9.V.85

This print is one of a set of ten produced by Mary Cassatt for her first exhibition at the Durand-Ruel
gallery in April 1891. They were inspired by Japanese woodblock prints and coloured *à la poupée*.

**Erich Heckel**
SELF PORTRAIT
Woodcut printed in colours by the artist on wove paper, signed in pencil and inscribed *III*,
1918, 18⅛in by 12¾in (46cm by 32.4cm)
New York $44,000 (£34,375). 8.XI.84

**Edvard Munch**
MADONNA — LIEBENDES WEIB
Lithograph printed in colours on wove paper, signed in pencil, 1895–1902,
sheet size 29⅝in by 25in (75.3cm by 63.4cm)
London £66,000 ($84,480). 5.XII.84

**Pablo Picasso**
LA MINOTAUROMACHIE
Etching, final state, signed and inscribed *une des trente épreuves du tirage*, 1935,
sheet size 20in by 30½in (50.7cm by 77.5cm)
London £137,500 ($176,000). 5.XII.84

*Opposite*
**Frank Stella**
CIRCUITS: TALLADEGA THREE II
Relief-printed etching in colours on dyed paper, signed in pencil, dated *1982*, from the edition of 30,
66in by 51½in (167.5cm by 131cm)
New York $31,900 (£24,922). 10.V.85·

# A daguerreotype portrait of the Duke of Wellington

## Terence Pepper

The record price paid on 26 October 1984 at Sotheby's for Claudet's sixth-plate daguerreotype of the Duke of Wellington (Fig. 1) reflects the remarkable interest of the item, not only as a rare historical document but also for its considerable importance as one of the earliest photographic portraits of an eminent sitter. Despite living well into the age of photography, the Duke's sitting to Claudet on his seventy-fifth birthday, 1 May 1844, is the only recorded instance of his being photographed. The daguerreotype sold at Sotheby's is one of two that survive from this sitting. As its containing case bears the address in Regent Street from which Claudet operated from 1851 onwards, it is possible that this image is a contemporary copy of the other, which remains in the collection of the present Duke at Stratfield Saye.

The daguerreotype process, by which an image is recorded and fixed on the sensitised silvered surface of a copper plate, was introduced in France by its inventor Louis-Jacques-Mandé Daguerre in 1839. Claudet learnt the process directly from Daguerre and became the first to practise the art in Britain. He was responsible for many improvements in the process, the most significant being the reduction in exposure time from minutes to seconds, thus increasing the possibilities of portraiture. Though financially less successful than his rival Richard Beard, Claudet nevertheless enjoyed a pre-eminent reputation for his artistic abilities. In 1856 a critic remarked in *The Athenaeum*, 'What Lawrence did with his brush M.Claudet appears to do with his lens; he catches the best aspect of his sitter and does full justice to nature. . . .'

Claudet's reputation and the relatively short time needed for a daguerreotype exposure, together with the prodigious public demand for likenesses of the Iron Duke must have been contributory factors in gaining the co-operation of the reluctant subject. Commenting on the Duke's dislike for sitting, his friend the Earl of Ellesmere is recorded as saying, 'I scarcely know a subject of which I should have so much feared to approach him'. An account of the sitting in *The Times* of 22 May 1845 records that the daguerreotype was placed in the hands of an artist, a Mr A. Solomon who used it as the basis for an enlarged portrait, now at Apsley House (Fig. 2). The painted portrait and the daguerreotype were then given to the engraver H.T.Ryall (Fig. 3). Such was the popularity of Claudet's image that subsequently many further portraits of the Duke were painted from the engraving, several being made posthumously on his death in 1852. In view of the rarity of the image and the comparative scarcity of the photographic technique it seems unlikely that a photograph of quite such interest will appear on the market for some time.

Fig. 1
**Antoine Claudet**
THE DUKE OF WELLINGTON
Sixth-plate daguerreotype, 1 May 1844
London £10,450 ($13,376). 26.X.84

*Below, right*
Fig. 2
**Abraham Solomon**, ARA
THE DUKE OF WELLINGTON
1845, 4½in by 3½in (11.5cm by 9cm)
Private collection. Reproduced courtesy of the Duke of
Wellington.

*Below, left*
Fig. 3
**Henry Thomas Ryall after Antoine Claudet**
FIELD MARSHAL THE DUKE OF WELLINGTON, KG
Engraving, 1845, image size 8¼in by 6⅜in
(20.8cm by 16.3cm)

# Photographs

**Hippolyte Bayard**
STUDY OF TWO ITEMS OF STATUARY
Direct positive on paper, inscribed in pencil
on the reverse *H.Bayard Essai de photographie
directe sur papier Mars-Avril 1839*,
3¾in by 2¾in (9.6cm by 6.8cm)
London £7,150 ($9,152). 26.X.84

This study is one of a group of seven
examples of Bayard's work rediscovered in
recent years. Bayard made his first recorded
experiments in late January 1839, after the
announcement on 7 January that year of the
invention of the daguerreotype process, but
before the details of Daguerre's methods
were published.

**Julia Margaret Cameron**
PORTRAIT OF MRS DUCKWORTH
Albumen print, *circa* 1867,
13⅞in by 10⅝in (35.2cm by 27cm)
London £14,300 ($18,304). 28.VI.85

*Furcellaria fastigiata.*

**Anna Atkins**
FURCELLARIA FASTIGIATA
*Photographs of British Algae*, one of a set of 211 cyanotype plates issued in parts from
October 1843, 10½in by 8¼in (26.5cm by 21cm)
London £48,400 ($61,952). 29.III.85
From the collection of John Herschel-Shorland

*British Algae*, the first scientific manual to be printed using photography instead of
typesetting and conventional means of illustration, predates Talbot's commercially
published photographic books. This set was given by Anna Atkins to Sir John Herschel,
inventor of the cyanotype process.

**Eugene Atget**
PROSTITUTE IN DOORWAY
Printing-out paper, numbered *11* by the photographer in
pencil and with the photographer's stamp on the reverse,
*circa* 1900–1905, 8½in by 6¾in (21.5cm by 17.1cm)
New York $19,250 (£15,039). 7.V.85
From the collection of Jean Levy

**André Kertesz**
AUX HALLES
Silver print, signed and dated *1929* on the mount and with
photographer's Paris studio stamp on the reverse,
6⅝in by 8¾in (16.9cm by 22.3cm)
New York $17,600 (£13,750). 5.XI.84

**Paul Outerbridge**
IDE COLLAR
Platinum print, 1922, 4⅝in by 3⅝in (11.8cm by 9.2cm)
New York $20,900 (£16,328). 7.V.85

This image was made for Geo.P.Ide & Co. and appeared in the November 1922 issue of *Vanity Fair* where it was seen by Marcel Duchamp in Paris. Attracted by the design, he fixed the page to his studio wall where it still hung three years later, when Outerbridge, with Man Ray, first visited Duchamp.

**Charles Sheeler**
STAIRWAY
Silver print, signed on the mount, 1935,
9⅜in by 6in (23.9cm by 15.2cm)
New York $37,400 (£29,219). 5.XI.84
From the collection of the late Constance Rourke

This image was made by Sheeler during a visit to Colonial Williamsburg, which inspired a series of photographs, drawings and paintings.

# Manuscripts and printed books

**Rufinus of Aquileia**
*Historia Ecclesiastica*, the Latin adaptation of the ecclesiastical chronicle of Eusebius of Caesarea, a bifolium from a manuscript on vellum, Ireland or Northumbria, early to mid-seventh century
London £82,500 ($105,600). 25.VI.85
From the collection of the Folger Shakespeare Library

This fragment was discovered in 1984 forming the outside wrapper of two sixteenth-century medical texts. It is written in the earliest type of Irish half-uncial script. If written by Irish scribes in Northumbria, as is likely, it is the oldest surviving manuscript produced in England.

**The Master of the Cypresses**
*Charity*, a cutting from an illuminated choirbook on vellum, perhaps by Pedro da Toledo, Seville,
*circa* 1435
London £36,300 ($46,464). 25.VI.85

**The Master of Charles V**
The Arenberg Missal, four of twenty-one miniatures from a manuscript on vellum, Antwerp,
*circa* 1520
London £319,000 ($408,320). 11.XII.84

This missal was painted in Antwerp for Marcus Cruyt, a Cistercian abbot and Imperial ambassador,
and afterwards belonged to the library of the Dukes of Arenberg

**The Master of Claude de France**
Book of Hours, *The Annunciation to the Shepherds*, one of fourteen large miniatures from a manuscript on vellum, Tours, *circa* 1515
London £264,000 ($337,920). 11.XII.84

# An Oriental 'old master'

## Margaret Erskine

Farrukh Beg, an Oriental 'old master', has long fascinated scholars of Indian miniature painting and a work by this celebrated artist, auctioned on 15 October 1984, caused great excitement in the field (Fig. 1). It bears an important historical inscription that not only determines the date of the artist's birth but confirms that he was highly regarded at the Mughal court, details rarely recorded on Indian minatures.

This hitherto unknown miniature depicts an elderly European surrounded by pet animals under a highly colourful and imaginative tree. Since the sale Dr Marianne Kuffner of C.G. Börner, Düsseldorf, has identified the European engraving on which the miniature is based. The composition is derived from an engraving by the Flemish artist Raphael Sadeler I (1560–circa 1630) after Marten de Vos, entitled *Dolor* (Fig. 2), one of a series of four allegorical prints, the first of which is dated 1591. Although Farrukh Beg has changed the background of the composition he was clearly inspired by this contemplative old man. In the top right-hand corner is an inscription stating that the work was painted in 1615 (AH 1024) in the artist's seventieth year. Written in a spidery hand, probably by the artist himself, it is of particular importance as it also tells us that Farrukh Beg was born in 1547 (AH 954–55), probably in Persia, and that he was honoured with the title *Nadir al-'asr*, 'Wonder of the age', by the Mughal emperor Jahangir. These two propositions were first set out by Robert Skelton, Keeper of the Indian department at the Victoria and Albert Museum, London, in an article published in *Ars Orientalis* nearly thirty years ago, but for which, until now, there has been no documentary evidence.

The Mughal court of the sixteenth and seventeenth centuries was a centre of artistic styles and influences. The empire in northern India had been founded by Babur (1483–1530), a direct descendant of Tamurlane and Ghengis Khan. Babur's son Humayun, a weak ruler who met an untimely death in 1556 falling from his library steps, had introduced Persian artists encountered during his exile in the Safavid court of Shah Tahmasp, when he was restored to Delhi in 1555. Humayun was succeeded by his son Akbar (1542–1605), a powerful Muslim ruler with eclectic tastes. He expanded the Mughal empire and continued to encourage foreigners of all creeds to visit his court. It seems likely that the Sadeler engraving found its way to the Mughal court through the Jesuit missions. Jerome Xavier (nephew of St Francis), who led the third mission to Lahore in 1595, stayed at the courts of Akbar and Jahangir for twenty-two years. Although every attempt to convert him to

Fig. 1
*An elderly scribe seated under a tree surrounded by pet animals,* by Farrukh Beg, dated 1615 (AH 1024)
London £71,500 ($91,520). 15.X.84

DOLOR

Fig. 2
*Dolor*, one of a series of four allegorical engravings by Raphael Sadeler I after Marten de Vos, *circa* 1591, 8⅝in by 8⅞in (22cm by 22.5cm)

Christianity failed, Akbar readily accepted gifts from Europe, including, in 1580, the great polyglot Bible published by Plantin in Antwerp. He also encouraged his court studio to copy European masters. It was by this broad-minded and cultured ruler, that Farrukh Beg was first acclaimed.

The arrival of Farrukh Beg at the Mughal court in 1585 is recorded by Abul Fazl, Akbar's prime minister and biographer, in the *Akbarnama*, the emperor's memoirs. The artist had travelled from Kabul to Lahore following the death of his patron Muhammad Hakim, Akbar's half-brother. During the latter years of Akbar's reign Farrukh Beg was commissioned to contribute to the decoration of the *Akbarnama*, *circa* 1595–1600, now in the Victoria and Albert Museum, and also to the *Khamsa* of Nizami, *circa* 1584–86, sold at Sotheby's in 1973, and now in the Keir Collection. He may also have spent several years at the Bijapuri court of Ibrahim Adil Shah II (1579–1627) in the Deccan, an independent Muslim kingdom further south. The present miniature, with its clear dating and strong Deccani influence, seen in the colourful tree and the fat-tailed sheep, adds powerful evidence for Farrukh Beg's connection with the Bijapuri style.

So highly valued was this miniature by the Mughals in the seventeenth century that it was mounted on a royal album page with exquisite floral borders and fine calligraphy, executed by one of the most accomplished of Mughal writing masters, and bears an attribution written by Shah Jahan, successor to Jahangir. The portrait is certainly one of the most important discoveries in the Indian miniature market in the last decade and confirms that this magnificent master, Farrukh Beg, was indeed worthy of his royal title, 'Wonder of the age'.

*Qur'an*, Arabic manuscript in *naskhi* script, Alexandria, third quarter
sixteenth century
London £44,000 ($56,320). 15.X.84
From the collection of the late King Umberto II of Italy

*Amir Hamze burning the armament chest of Zoroaster*, a page from the Mughal emperor Akbar's
copy of the *Hamza-nama, circa* 1570
London £148,500 ($190,080). 16.IV.85

*Opposite*
*The Imam Ali bin Abi Taleb beheading Nasr bin al-Hareth in the presence of the Prophet Muhammed*,
a page from a Turkish manuscript of Darir's *Siyar-i Nabi* (*The Life of the Prophet*),
Constantinople, *circa* 1594
London £46,200 ($59,136). 15.IV.85

عرف الظبیه منزلنه قوندلر رسول حضرت علیه السلام بیورد یکم
عقبه بن ابی معیط حاضر ایلدیلر بینی عجلاق دندن عبدالله بن سلمه

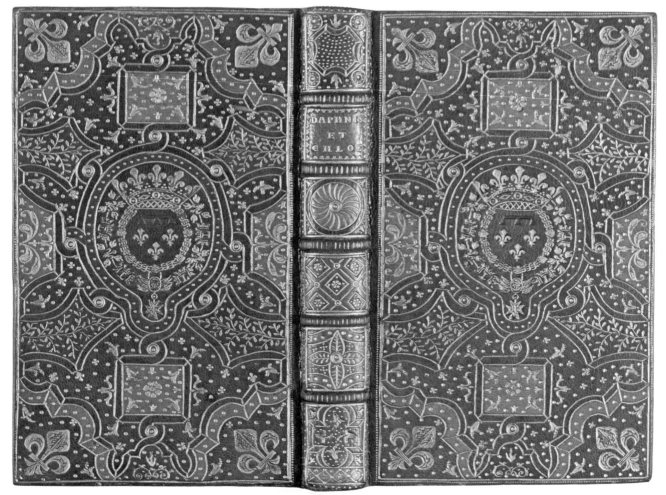

**Longus**
*Les amours pastorales de Daphnis et Chloë*, bound in mosaic morocco and embossed with the arms of
Philippe d'Orléans, with a frontispiece by Coypel and thirteen double-page plates engraved by
B. Audran, Quillau, Paris, 1718
Monte Carlo FF 832,500 (£69,375:$88,847). 12.XII.84

*Opposite*
**William Shakespeare**
*Comedies, Histories and Tragedies*, first folio edition, London, 1623
New York $638,000 (£498,438). 24.IV.85
From the collection of the late Paul Francis Webster

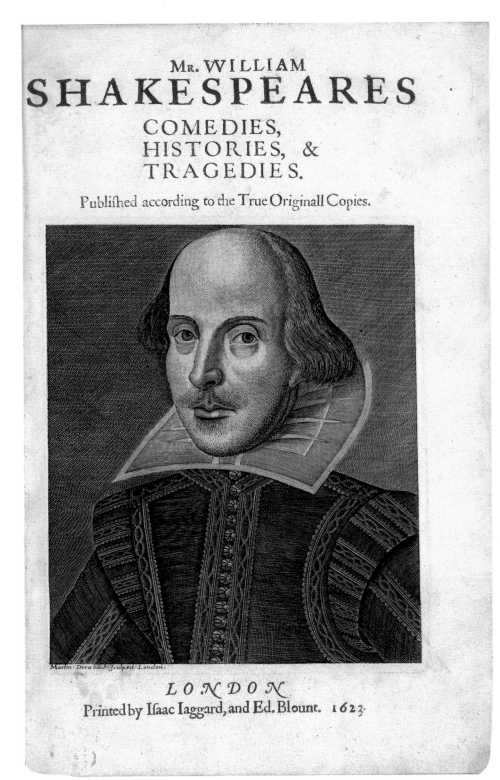

Mr. WILLIAM

# SHAKESPEARES

COMEDIES,
HISTORIES, &
TRAGEDIES.

Publiſhed according to the True Originall Copies.

Martin Droeshout sculpsit London.

*LONDON*
Printed by Iſaac Iaggard, and Ed. Blount. 1623.

**John Gould**
*The Birds of Australia*, first edition,
eight volumes, 681 hand-coloured
lithographed plates by Elizabeth Gould
and H.C. Richter after John Gould,
published by the author, London,
[1840]–1869
New York $82,500 (£64,453). 2.II.85

PLATYCERCUS SPLENDIDUS; Gould.

*Opposite*
**William Blake – Edward Young**
*The Complaint and the Consolation, or Night Thoughts*, forty-three pictorial borders designed, engraved
and hand-coloured by William Blake, R. Noble for R. Edwards, London, 1797
London £13,750 ($17,600). 17.XII.84

**Heirs of Johann Baptista Homann**
*Städt-Atlas*, engraved title, ninety-five double-page engraved maps and plans, hand-coloured throughout, Nuremberg, 1762
London £41,800 ($53,504). 2.V.85

**Johannes van Keulen**
*De Groote Nieuwe Vermeerderde Zee-Atlas ofte Water-Werelt*, engraved allegorical title by Aernout Naghtegael after Jan Luyken, 160 hand-coloured engraved sea and coastal charts, maps and a plan of Amsterdam, Amsterdam, *circa* 1695–1700
London £46,200 ($59,136). 20.IX.84

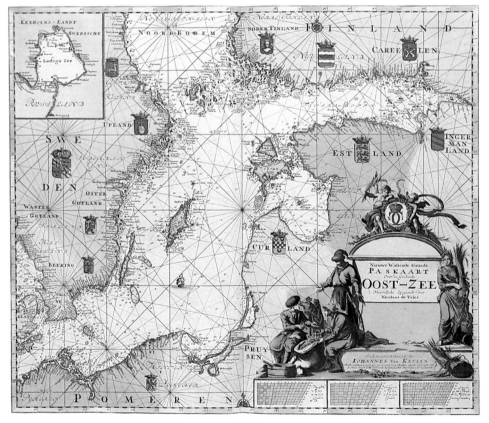

**Petrus Apianus**
*Astronomicum Caesareum*, fifty-nine leaves with
thirty-six hand-coloured woodcuts, published by the
author, Ingolstadt, May 1540
New York $88,000 (£68,750). 2.II.85

**Tycho Brahe**
*Astronomiae instauratae mechanica*, first edition, presentation
copy inscribed by the author to Pietro Duodo, five
engraved and twenty-six woodcut plates, hand-
coloured throughout, Philip de Ohr, Wandesbeck, 1598
London £57,200 ($73,216). 27.VI.85

From 1599–1602 Pietro Duodo was Venetian ambassador
to the court of Emperor Rudolph II at Prague. There he
met Tycho Brahe who had arrived at the Imperial court
in 1600, the year before he died.

No 191

201

*Charles R*

Charles by the Grace of God King of England,
Scotland, France and Ireland, Defendor of the
Faith &c.   To all Our loving Subjects of what degree
or quality soever, Greeting.   If the generall Distracti-
on and Confusion which is spread over the whole King-
dome, doth not awaken all men to a desire and longing that
those Wounds which haue so many yeares together been
kept bleeding may be bound up, all We can say will
be to noe purpose; However after this long Silence
We haue thought it Our Duty to Declare how much
We desire to contribute thereunto; and that as We
can never give over the hope in good time to obteyne
the possession of that Right, wch God and Nature
hath made Our Due; soe We doe make it Our dayly
Suete to the Devine Providence, That he will in Com-
passion to Vs and Our Subjects, after so long misery
& sufferings, remitt and put Vs into a quiet & peace-
able possession of that Our Right with as little blood
and dammage to Our People, as is possible: Nor doe
We desire more to enjoy what is Ours, then that

*Right*
The archive of Charles Townley (1737–1805), comprising correspondence and papers and engravings concerning Townley's collection of classical antiquities, several thousand pages
London £187,000 ($239,360). 23.VII.85
From the collection of Lord O'Hagan

*Opposite*
**Charles II**
The Declaration of Breda, the signed and sealed manuscript proclaiming the restoration of the British monarchy, four pages, Breda, 4–14 April 1660
London £93,500 ($119,680). 23.VII.85
From the collection of the late Earl of Sandwich 1943 Settlement

*Below*
One of two watercolours showing Charles Townley's collection at Park Street, Westminster, *circa* 1793, 15½in by 21in (39.4cm by 53.3cm)
London £57,200 ($73,216). 23.VII.85
From the collection of Lord O'Hagan

The watercolour can be dated by the presence of the Discobolus, which had been found in the ruins of Hadrian's Villa in 1791 and was purchased by Townley in 1792.

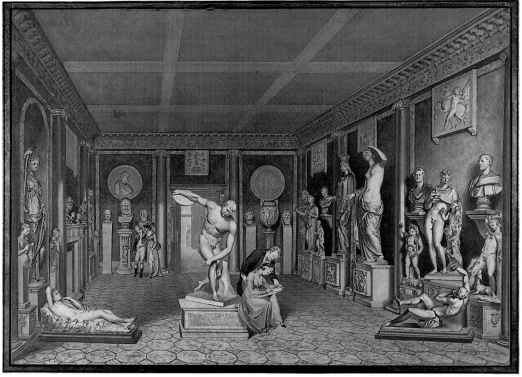

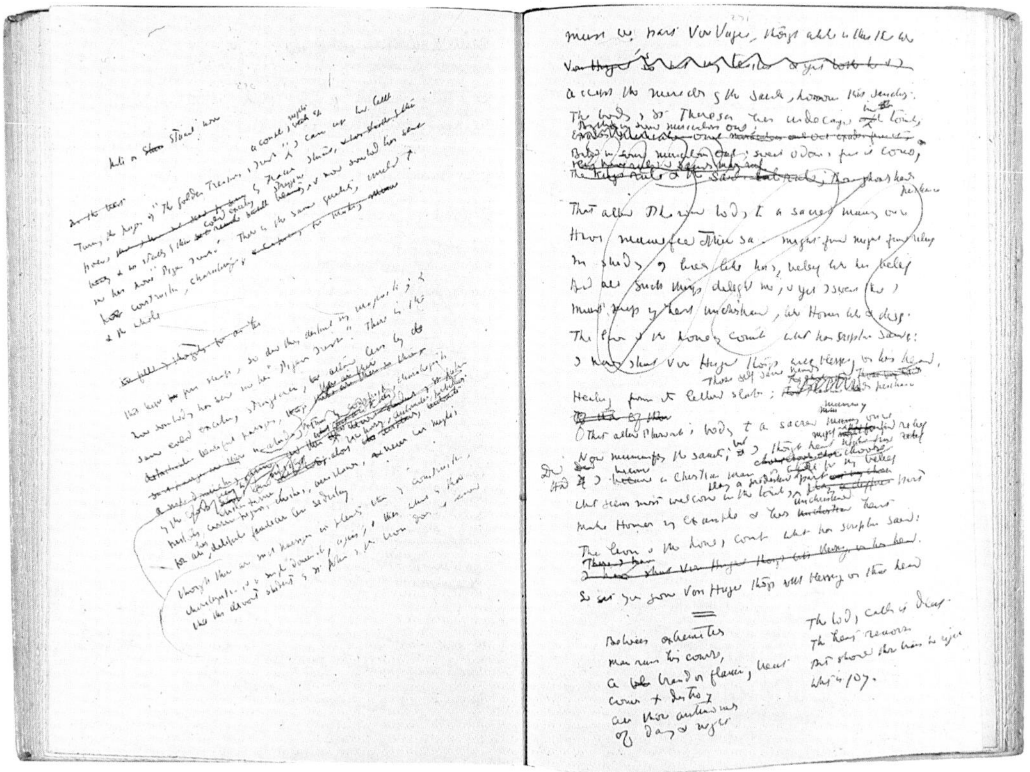

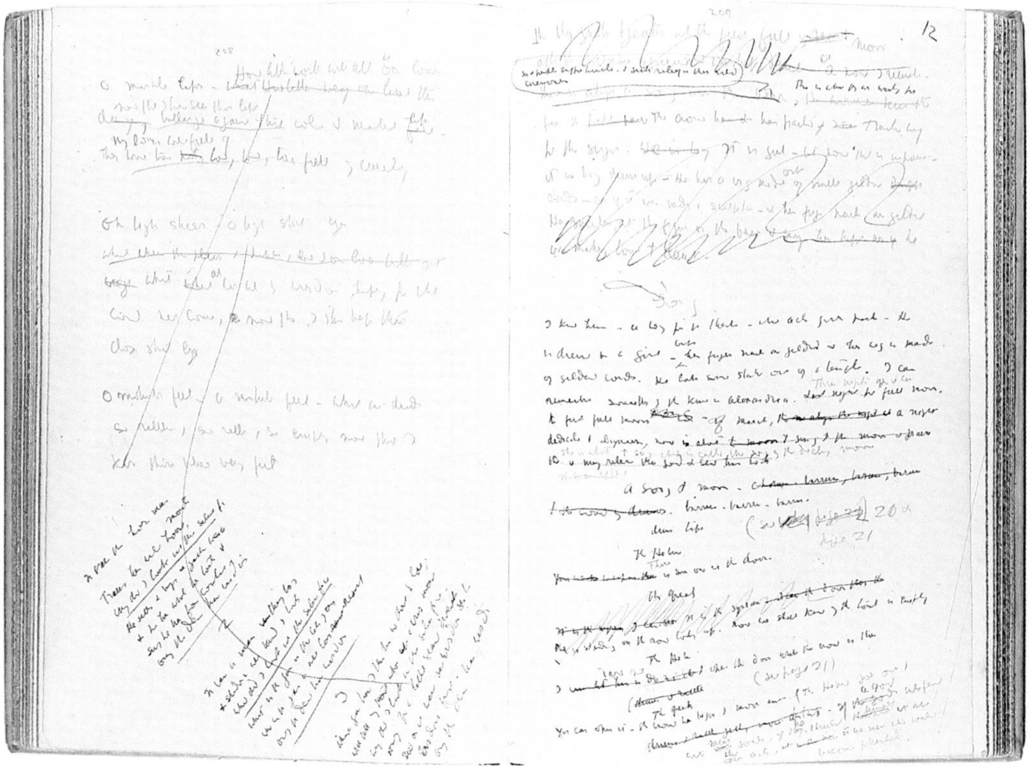

**Robert Schumann**
An autograph manuscript of the first movement of the *Phantasie in C major Op. 17*, signed twice,
twelve pages, *circa* 1838–39
London £88,000 ($112,640). 23.XI.84

This is a working manuscript with numerous corrections, alterations and deletions. The *Phantasie* was
begun at the start of Schumann's romantic attachment to Clara Wieck, to whom he wrote that it was
'the most passionate thing I ever composed – a deep lament for you'. The work was also composed as
a tribute to Beethoven.

*Opposite*
**William Butler Yeats**
The great vellum notebook containing autograph drafts of poetry and prose, folio, 387 pages,
23 November 1930–mid-1933
London £275,000 ($352,000). 22.VII.85
From the collection of Michael Yeats

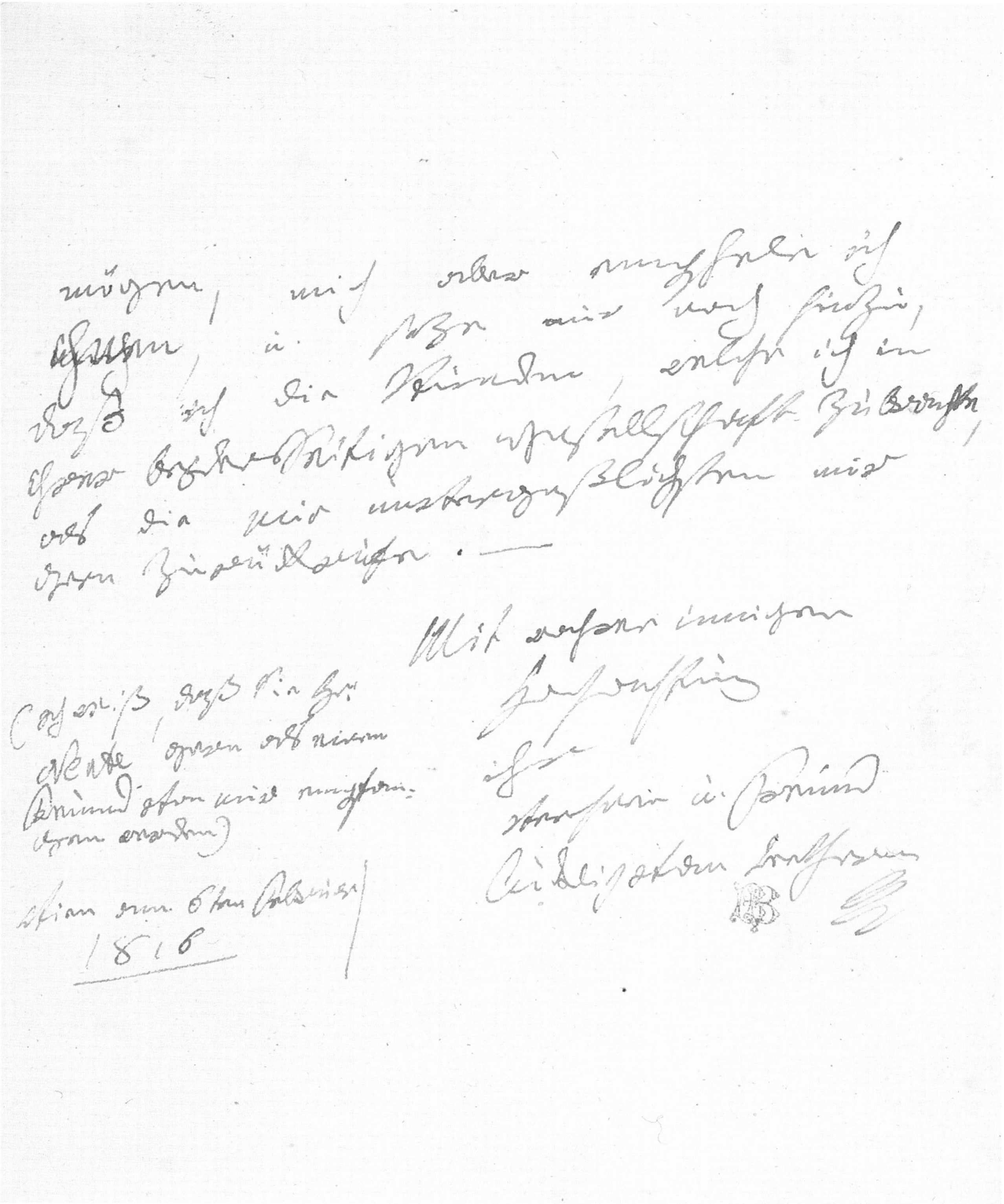
1816

**Richard Strauss**
An autograph manuscript of *Malven*,
signed and inscribed to Maria Jeritza,
two pages, Montreux,
23 November 1948
New York $60,500 (£47,266).
12.XII.84
From the collection of the late
Maria Jeritza Seery

This manuscript is the only known
complete copy of Strauss' last song,
sent by the composer to Maria Jeritza,
one of the greatest interpreters of his
music.

*Opposite*
**Ludwig van Beethoven**
An autograph letter to Antonie Brentano, enclosing an engraving of the composer by Blasius Höfel,
three pages, Vienna, 6 February 1816
London £55,000 ($70,400). 9.V.85

Antonie Brentano, to whom Beethoven dedicated his 'Diabelli Variations' in 1823, is believed to have
been the composer's 'Immortal Beloved'.

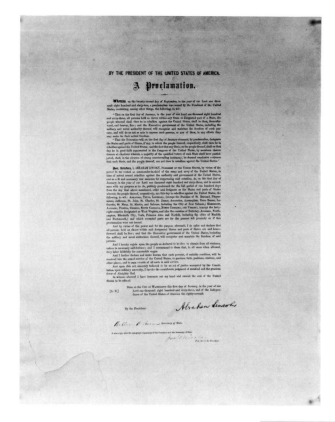

**Abraham Lincoln**

A broadside copy of the Emancipation Proclamation, signed, one page, Washington DC, 1 January 1863
New York $297,000 (£232,031). 31.X.84

*Opposite*

**Abraham Lincoln**

A photograph of Lincoln and his son Tad, signed by the President for himself and his son, taken at Matthew Brady's Washington studio, 9 February 1864
New York $104,500 (£81,641). 27.III.85
From the collection of Mrs Philip D. Sang

**George Washington**

A letter, signed, to Major Benjamin Tallmadge discussing the operation of a spy ring in British headquarters in New York, three and a half pages, West Point, 24 September 1779
New York $121,000 (£94,531). 31.X.84

# The Crahan Collection of books on food and related subjects

Fanny Mallary

Marcus Crahan, a Los Angeles physician, became interested in both food and wine and in rare books while at medical school. He combined these interests in a collection formed over thirty years, assisted by his wife Elizabeth, herself a medical librarian. The Crahan's collecting was not confined to books on food and wine but extended to subjects that concerned every aspect of the production and enjoyment of food and drink. Thus, their library contained books on farming, including André Simon's copy of Pietro Crescentio's *Ruralia commoda* (Fig. 1), the first printed work on agriculture, and books on bee-keeping, hunting and fishing, medicine, dining and so forth. Both the Crahans were tremendously interested in what they termed 'the art of life', and this was reflected in their collection, in such curiosities as a manuscript ledger (Fig. 2) of the menus served to Queen Victoria's household at Windsor.

The collection contained an impressive number of the classic rarities, including the second edition of the first printed cookery book, Platina's *De honesta voluptate et valetudine*, Venice, 1475, ($39,600); the first edition of the earliest surviving cookery text, the work of the Roman gourmet Apicius *De re Coquinaria*, Milan, 1498, ($25,300) and Cristoforo di Messisbugo's account of the banquets held at the Este court *Banchetti Compositione di Vivande* (Fig. 3). There were classics of French cookery like *Le Pastissier François*, printed in Amsterdam by the Elzeviers in 1655 ($14,300) and one of the most sought-after of rare cookery books, La Varenne's *Le Cuisinier François*, Paris, 1651 ($8,250); *L'Art du cuisinier*, Paris, 1814, by Antoine Beauvilliers, the first of the great French chef-restauranteurs ($3,575) and Brillat-Savarin's celebrated work on the philosophy of gastronomy, *La Physiologie du goût*, Paris, 1826 ($2,860). The Crahans also owned four editions of Hannah Glasse's *The Art of Cookery Made Plain and Easy*, including the Bute copy of the 1747 first edition ($6,600). Dr Johnson referred to Mrs Glasse's work when he claimed that 'women can spin very well; but they cannot make a good book of cookery.' Nevertheless it was the most successful English cookery book for one hundred years after its appearance.

The earliest cookery books printed in America were imported English texts and it was only in 1796 that the first native American cookery book, Amelia Simmons's *American Cookery*, appeared. It contained the first printed recipes for such American specialities as Indian pudding and johnnycake. Early editions of the work are

Fig. 1
**Pietro Crescentio**
*Ruralia commoda*, first edition, bound in contemporary
blind-stamped brass-embossed red sheep over wood
boards. Augsburg, 1471
New York $31,900 (£24,922). 9.X.84
From the Crahan Collection

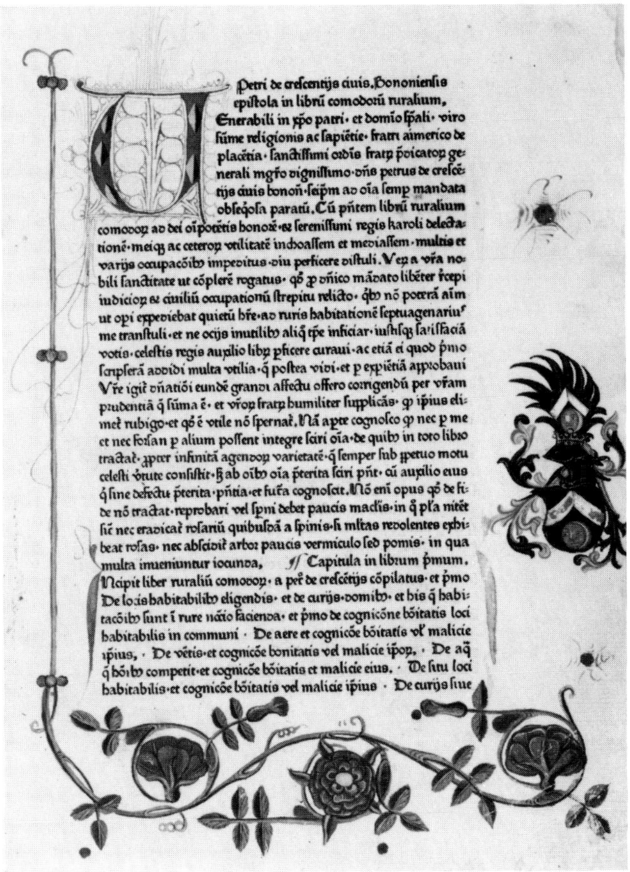

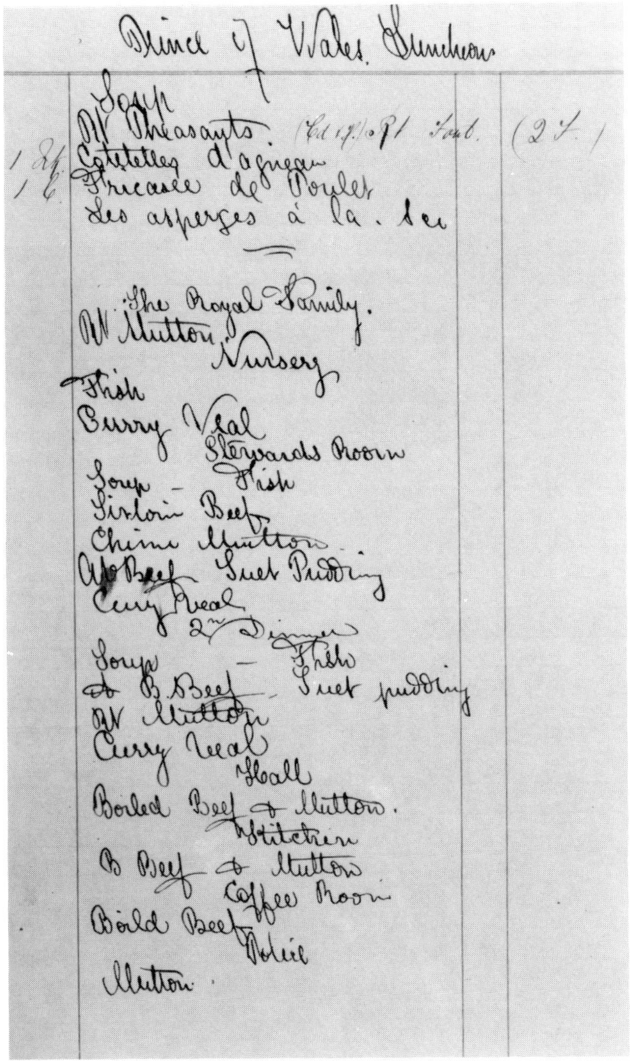

Fig. 2
A manuscript ledger listing menus served to the
royal household of Queen Victoria, Windsor Castle,
31 August 1863–12 January 1864
New York $23,100 (£18,047). 10.X.84
From the Crahan Collection

Fig. 3
**Cristoforo di Messisbugo**
*Banchetti Compositione di Vivande, et Apparecchio generale*,
first edition, two large woodcut illustrations,
containing menus and recipes for banquets held at
the Este court from 1524–48, Ferrara, 1549
New York $14,300 (£11,172). 9.X.84
From the Crahan Collection

extremely rare; the Crahans' copy of the Hartford, 1798 third edition is one of only eight known copies of the first three editions.

While it is understandable that rare books should make extraordinary prices, no one could have predicted the success of less well-known titles. English cookery books did well, such as John Shirley's *The Accomplished Ladies Rich Closet of Rarieties* (Fig. 4), embellished with a delightful historiated title-page showing seventeenth-century ladies engaged in various household activities, and Maria Ward's *The Complete Cook-Maid or Housewife's Assistant* (Fig. 5), which is the only recorded copy of this book. Regional American cookery books, also attracted attention: *What Mrs Fisher Knows about Old Southern Cooking*, with recipes dictated by an illiterate former-slave and published in San Francisco in 1881 made $2,640 and the first cookery book printed in Los Angeles, a slim compilation of recipes put out by the Ladies' Aid Society of the Fort Street Church made $6,050.

The Crahan sale offered 786 lots containing some 1500 books on a wide variety of subjects, and realised a grand total of $875,605. Although prices were strong overall, the cookery books provoked the greatest competition. Bidding was brisk among dealers and collectors from Europe and the States but was dominated by the representatives of a single private collector who bought two-thirds of the collection.

Fig. 4
**John Shirley**
*The Accomplished Ladies Rich Closet of Rarities or the Ingenious Gentlewoman &*
*Servant Maids Delightfull Companion*, first edition, engraved title and one
full-page illustration, London, 1687
New York $11,000 (£8,594). 9.X.84
From the Crahan Collection

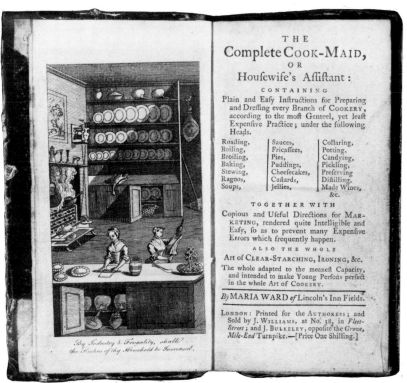

Fig. 5
**Maria Ward**
*The Complete Cook-Maid, or Housewife's Assistant*, engraved frontispiece,
London, *circa* 1766
New York $7,150 (£5,586). 9.X.84
From the Crahan Collection

# Coins and medals

*Left*
Insignia of a Knight Grand Cross of the
Guelphic Order of Hanover awarded to
Vice-Admiral Sir Richard Dacres, GCH
London £4,950 ($6,336). 27.VI.85

*Right*
A group of medals and insignia awarded to Field-Marshal
Sir Richard Dacres, GCB
London £8,800 ($11,264). 27.VI.85

Sir Richard Dacres, the elder son of Vice-Admiral Sir Richard Dacres
(see *left*), commanded the British artillery and directed the bombardment
of Sebastopol during the Crimean War.

A group of orders and decorations
awarded to Major-General Sir William
Williams, KCB, for his service in Spain
during the Peninsular War, 1808–1812
London £16,500 ($21,120). 1.XI.84

A group of medals awarded to Commander J.R. Stenhouse, RNR
London £4,620 ($5,914). 27.VI.85
From the collection of Mrs J.P. Mantell

These medals were awarded for services during the Great War and on Sir Ernest Shackleton's
Trans-Antarctic Expedition of 1914–16. Stenhouse commanded the expedition's ship *Aurora* and
eventually brought her safely back to New Zealand. Shackleton later wrote that Stenhouse had
'accomplished successfully one of the most difficult journeys on record, in an ocean area notoriously
stormy and treacherous.'

**Portugal**, Morabitino of Sancho I
(1185–1211)
London £6,820 ($8,730). 16.V.85

**Portugal**, português of
Manuel I (1495–1521)
London £19,800 ($25,344).
16.V.85

**Portugal**, peça of Maria II,
1833
London £3,520 ($4,506).
16.V.85

**Portugal**, moeda of João V, 1712, Porto mint
London £7,920 ($10,138). 16.V.85

**Portugal**, engenhoso of Sebastião, 1566
London £10,120 ($12,954). 16.V.85

**India**, Mughal, muhur of Jahangir,
regnal year 6 (AD 1611)
Geneva SFr 14,300 (£4,320:$5,521).
25.VI.85

**Abbasid Caliphate**, dinar of Abu'l-'Abbas
Ahmad al-Musta'in billah, AH 248
(AD 862), Makka mint
Geneva SFr 55,000 (£16,616:$21,236).
25.VI.85

**Ancient Greece**, Caria,
tetradrachm of Knidos, 390–340 BC
London £3,740 ($4,787). 25.X.84

**Austria**, Bishopric of Olmutz,
half-thaler struck in gold of Charles
III of Lorraine (1695–1711)
Zurich SFr 22,000
(£6,647:$8,494). 24.I.85

**Germany**, Nuremberg,
presentation 12 ducats or thaler
struck in gold, 1745
Zurich SFr 67,100
(£20,272:$25,907). 25.I.85

**Germany**, House of Neuenahr,
thaler klippe of Adolph von
Alpheim, 1583
Zurich SFr 20,350
(£6,148:$7,857). 25.I.85

*Left and right*
**Austria**, Archbishopric of Salzburg,
medallic double-thaler struck in gold
of Johann Jakob Khuen von Belasi,
1571
Zürich SFr 93,500
(£28,248:$36,100). 24.I.85

The coins on this page are from the Virgil M. Brand Collection.

# Insights into the Brand Collection

David Enders Tripp

Over the past three years Sotheby's has been privileged to offer the foreign and ancient coins that formed part of the collection assembled by Virgil Michael Brand (Fig. 1). The series of ten sales, concluded in October 1985, has resulted in some remarkable statistics. The total amount realised, in excess of £4.5 million, is by far the greatest sum ever made for a single owner collection of foreign and ancient coins. Indeed, in their entirety, the estate's numismatic holdings represented but a fraction of what was once the largest and most valuable collection ever formed by an individual. That the series of sales has been such a resounding success, in what has been an otherwise uncertain numismatic market, is due to the collection's content, the outstanding provenance and, perhaps most significantly, the fact that these coins had not been seen for more than sixty years.

While Virgil Brand, a somewhat eccentric Chicago brewer, has long been acknowledged by numismatists as the single greatest collector of coins, he has otherwise remained virtually unknown, yet he must rank among America's greatest art collectors. Indeed, the Mellons, Walters, Rockefellers, Fricks, Havemeyers and Morgans were perhaps less significant to their chosen areas of collecting than Virgil Brand was to his. It is to some extent the highly personal nature of coin collecting that has prevented a wider acknowledgement of his accomplishments. At the time of his death the collection numbered some 368,000 specimens. Amassed over a period of thirty-seven years, at a cost exceeding two million dollars, it was unparalleled by any individual and by few museums.

With a collection of such dimensions, the question that inevitably arises is, was Brand a collector or a hoarder? Brand was most certainly the former: his expertise was acknowledged and there are various published accounts of some of his more important discoveries. His general numismatic knowledge must have been awesome, for each specialised segment of his collection was in itself an important and comprehensive cabinet. Those areas that received his most especial interest included the issues of Germany, the United States, France, Italy, Britain and Ancient Greece and Rome. And, as would be expected of such a Maecenas, he opened his collection to the leading scholars of the period.

Calling on his initial training as a book-keeper, Brand personally kept his acquisitions ledgers in which he described the salient characteristics of each purchase (Fig. 2).

Fig. 1
Virgil M. Brand
(1861–1926)

These listings were often detailed and, in addition to the date, denomination and country of origin, included references to the standard works of the period. If he was sceptical of the attribution or authenticity of a specimen this too found its way into the ledgers and, in every case, whether by auction or by private treaty, the price as well as from whom the coin was purchased was diligently noted. The ledgers have fortunately survived and have recently been reunited as a group after more than fifty years. They provide a unique view of the formation of the collection.

Through these volumes we can chart Mr Brand's waxing and waning of specialised interests; his periods of concentrated attention to certain series and his sudden lack of interest in others. We can also determine just how wisely or well he bought. There were specimens for which he developed such a keen desire that his better judgement was clouded and the resulting over-payment was enormous. Then again, his pure instinct, encyclopaedic knowledge and substantial pocket allowed for gambles, which time has proved to have been sound. But both the mistakes and triumphs only serve to emphasise that the hunt and ultimate possession were the prime objectives.

Up until 1909 Brand's methods of forming and expanding his collection were fairly conventional. He maintained a high profile; the frequent appearance of his name in numismatic publications testifies to his purchasing power. He is known to have frequented some of the major sales held in the United States; it is not known, however, if he ever attended any of the European sales held at this time. For reasons unknown, around 1910 his habits changed; he became reclusive, references to him in publications are almost non-existent and it is not known if he ever again attended a sale. He continued to buy at public auctions, occasionally employing a dealer as agent, but often submitting bids by wire or by mail. It has been reported that so pivotal were his bids to the success of a sale that, pending their arrival, auctions would simply be postponed. In the meantime the dealers, who had long been his suppliers, continued to keep him busy. He received large shipments of coins, from which he kept what he wanted, or indeed the entire group. To the many European dealers who, accompanied by vast trunks of coins, made one or two special trips to Chicago a year, Mr Brand's collecting thirst must have seemed unquenchable.

The ultimate disposition of the collection was as complex as its many parts. During Brand's lifetime the American Numismatic Society in New York, which today houses the finest collection of coins in the United States, made a truly astounding offer: they proposed building a separate wing, not only to house the coins, but Mr Brand as well! Although the proposition was refused it testifies to the importance with which numismatists viewed the collection.

When Brand died intestate in 1926 the coins passed to his two brothers, Armin and Horace. They attempted to sell them to the United States Government, to form a national coin collection. The asking price was the cost plus simple interest for the thirty-seven-year period the collection took to form. Their offer was refused, for which their heirs must be grateful but scholars must lament.

Unable to find any one individual purchaser for the entire collection, it was split evenly in half, by both value and content, and effectively each brother spent the remainder of his life living off this huge accumulation. By 1962, when Horace Brand died, only a tiny percentage of the collection remained in family hands. It is that portion, willed by Armin Brand to his daughter Jane in 1946, and held until her death in 1981, that has excited the numismatic market for the past few years.

What then is the measure of a great collection? Today it is all too often taken to be its sale value. The 'numbers' game has been played with the Brand Collection for years and, although estimates vary, it is generally accepted that had the collection survived intact its value would have probably exceeded one billion dollars.

The more important measure of greatness should be the content of the collection. Although the monumental rarities, those pieces better known to the general public, were long gone, museums, national and local have competed at virtually every Brand auction for the opportunity to fill the gaps in their collections. In this regard it is a tribute to the collector that so rich were his holdings that even in the comparatively small remaining fraction sold at Sotheby's between 1982 and 1985 rarities of astounding importance should still abound.

Fig. 2
Virgil Brand's acquisitions ledger,
volume 20, open at the page listing
purchases from the Geheimrat S
Collection. These included fifty lots
offered by Sotheby's, Zurich,
24–25 January 1985, Brand
Part VIII.

*Left*
**India**, East India Company, proof
two mohurs struck in silver, 1854, the reverse
depicting a lion standing before a palm,
probably by W. or L.C. Wyon after
John Flaxman
London £3,080 ($3,942). 14.VI.85
From the Virgil M. Brand Collection

*Right*
**Jamaica**, gold doubloon, *circa* 1758, a
1751 Lima mint 8 escudos bearing the
countermark *GR* for George II of
England
London £18,700 ($23,936). 14.VI.85
From the Virgil M. Brand Collection

The coins on this page were purchased for Virgil M. Brand from the 'Nobleman' (Count Ferrari)
Collection, the British and British colonial portions of which were sold by Sotheby's,
27–31 March 1922.

# Arms and armour

A William and Mary military cap, *circa* 1690
London £7,150 ($9,152). 2.X.84

The cap bears the cypher of both William and Mary and must therefore date from before Mary's death in 1694. The design omits the English rose, which may indicate that the cap came from a Scottish regiment serving with the Dutch forces.

A three-quarter armour for a cuirassier, *circa* 1640
London £5,500 ($7,040). 23.IV.85

A 12-bore sidelock ejector gun by John Wilkes, the action and furniture engraved with a woodcock plumage design by Malcolm Appleby, completed 1983
Houston $17,600 (£13,750). 15.XI.84

Malcolm Appleby's metal engraving breaks away from the traditional motifs associated with the ornament of sporting guns, introducing decorative themes that complement the function of the gun.

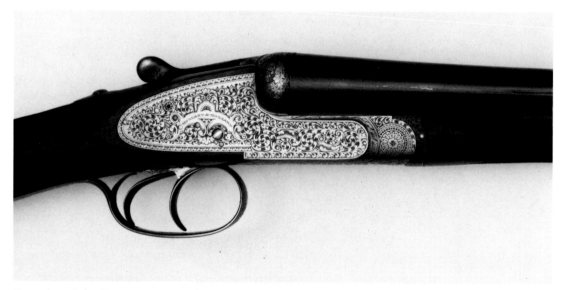

One of a pair of 'Royal Brevis' 12-bore self-opening detachable sidelock ejector guns by Holland & Holland, *circa* 1937
Pulborough £23,650 ($30,272). 24.IV.85

A 12-bore hammer ejector gun by J. Purdey & Sons, number two of a pair built for Lord Ripon
(as Earl de Grey) in 1895; with the game book (1893–1929) of Charles Julian, Lord Ripon's head
keeper at Studley Royal
Pulborough £14,300 ($18,304). 24.IV.85
From the collection of J.F. Julian, Charles Julian's son

A lightweight 12-bore self-opening sidelock ejector gun by J. Purdey & Sons, 1932
Pulborough £10,450 ($13,376). 24.IV.85

# Judaica

A German parcel-gilt silver Hanukah lamp, probably by Johann Christoph Hoening, Augsburg, 1763–65, height 9in (22.9cm)
New York $57,750 (£45,117). 26.VI.85

**Isidore Kaufmann**
THE DESCENDANT OF THE HIGH PRIEST
On panel, signed, 16in by 12in (40.7cm by 30.5cm)
New York $132,000 (£103,125). 6.XII.84

# Hebrew manuscripts from the Sassoon Collection

## Professor Chimen Abramsky

Since November 1975 the remarkable collection of Hebrew manuscripts formed by the late Mr David Sassoon have been sold through Sotheby's in four parts. The first two sales, when thirty-eight and thirty-three manuscripts, respectively, were sold in Zürich, took place in November 1975 and November 1978. At the third sale in New York in May 1981 one hundred and one manuscripts were dispersed and the fourth part of the collection, comprising ninety-seven manuscripts, was sold in New York on 4 December 1984. All four sales attracted world-wide attention because of the reputation of the collector's scholarship, the quality of the manuscripts and the rich diversity of the subjects covered.

The late Mr David Sassoon (1880–1942) was born in Bombay, a member of one of the most eminent aristocratic Jewish families of the Far East. The family traced its descent from an illustrious Spanish Jewish family that migrated to Baghdad after the expulsion of the Jews from Spain in 1492. The Sassoon family established themselves as financiers, first in Baghdad and, from the second half of the eighteenth century, in Bombay and Calcutta. From the mid-nineteenth century, many members of the family settled in England where their distinguished public and philanthropic services were honoured.

David Sassoon was the only member of his family to be deeply devoted both to religion and to scholarship. Having started collecting at the early age of thirteen, as a young man he travelled widely in the East and through Europe searching for rare manuscripts and printed books. The latter were sold by Sotheby's in London during 1970–71. From 1894 until his death in 1942, David Sassoon amassed over thirteen hundred Hebrew and Samaritan manuscripts embracing virtually the whole spectrum of the Jewish literary heritage, from the Bible, Mishna, Talmud, Midrashim, medieval Hebrew poetry (in which Sassoon himself specialised), philosophy, mysticism, medicine, astronomy, rabbinic law, lexicography and grammar, liturgy, Samaritan Bibles and, last but not least, exceptional illuminated Hebrew manuscripts. In 1932 he published, through the Oxford University Press, a magnificent two-volume catalogue of his collection covering 1152 manuscripts, providing detailed descriptions

Fig. 1
**Moshe ben Maimon**
*The Great Halachic Code of Maimonides with glosses of Rabbi Meir Ha'Cohen*, a Hebrew
manuscript in Ashkenazi square script and rabbinic cursive script on vellum, copied
by Yakov ben Joseph Ha'Levi, Germany, dated December 1355 – January 1356
[16th Tebet (5) 116]
New York $451,000 (£352, 344). 4.XII.84
From the Sassoon Collection

with extracts in Hebrew of the important texts, indices of authors, titles, owners, and place names, augmented by seventy-two plates. The work was acclaimed as an invaluable contribution to scholarship.

The sales of the Sassoon Collection have all held exceptional items. Some outstandingly rare texts were among the ninety-seven Hebrew manuscripts sold in New York in December 1984, when others of interest to collectors, scholars and academic institutions alike were also dispersed. The manuscripts testified to the richness and diversity of Jewish culture and creativity through the centuries, reflecting the intellectual activity of Jews in Spain, Italy, Germany, the Near East and of scattered communities of the Far East, such as the Benei Israel and Cochin Jews of India.

Of particular interest were a miscellany of philosophic and kabbalistic tracts from Greece, dated 1468, which sold for $19,800; an anonymous commentary in Hebrew from Spain on the Pesachim Talmudic tractate of the Babylonian Talmud of 1416 ($23,100); the *Decisions on rabbinic law* of Isiah Di Trani the Elder, who lived in southern Italy in the thirteenth century ($33,000), while his grandson's legal decisions from 1393 sold for $110,000. The text of the latter provides an insight into the conditions of the Jews in Italy at that date and touches extensively on commercial contacts with the Christian population. A small Spanish prayerbook with primitive illustrations from the fourteenth century sold for $137,500, while a festival prayerbook, also written in Spanish and illustrated by Iehuda Machabeulo in Amsterdam in 1659, sold for $110,000. It was written for the 'New Christians', the Marranos, who escaped the clutches of the Spanish Inquisition and fled to Holland where they returned to Judaism. The scribe was the greatest Jewish graphic artist of the seventeenth century. One of the rarest items was a folio of well over one thousand leaves, the *Mishne Torah*, Maimonides' great rabbinic code, rich in textual variants, which was copied in Germany in 1356, with a commentary by the German Rabbi Meir Ha'Cohen (Fig. 1).

Undoubtedly the two outstanding items were illuminated manuscripts; the first a treatise on astronomy by the Spanish Jewish astronomer Yakov ben David ben Yomtov Fual, written in Spain *circa* 1360–61, with many illuminations in the best style of medieval manuscript illumination. The second was a model codex of the Hebrew Bible, written and exquisitely illuminated in Soria, Spain in 1312 by the foremost rabbinic authority of the time, Shem Tov ben Abraham Gaon (Fig. 2). The Rabbi-scribe was a distinguished member of a well-known family of artist-scribes (his brother illuminated manuscripts now held in the British Library and in the Irish University Library). This sumptuous Bible from the fourteenth century is one of the most important Hebrew Bibles in the world.

Until the sale of Sassoon's collection of printed books and manuscripts Hebrew books were treated by the major auction houses as of limited value; the step-children of Western manuscripts. Now the catalogues are recognised in the Jewish scholarly world as major works of reference, meticulously prepared, providing up-to-date bibliographical references on the lots offered for sale. David Sassoon would have appreciated this change in emphasis, affirmed by the value placed on his collection.

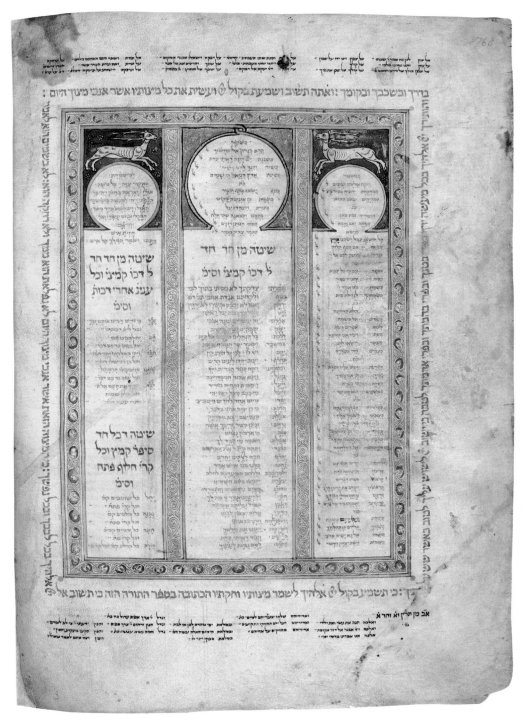

Fig. 2
*The Shem Tov ben Abraham Gaon Bible*, a Hebrew manuscript in Spanish square script on vellum, Soria, Spain, dated 1312 [(5) 072]
New York $825,000 (£644,531). 4.XII.84
From the Sassoon Collection

# Works of art

A Limoges enamel and copper-gilt reliquary châsse, early thirteenth century, height 9¾in (24.8cm)
New York $264,000 (£206,250). 21.V.85
From the collection of Jack and Belle Linsky

A Saxon gold and enamel chain of office and medallion of the household of Christian II,
reigned 1591–1611, height of medallion 2¼in (5.7cm)
London £66,000 ($84,480). 2.IV.85

*Centre*
A German gold double-portrait medallion of Johann Georg I of Saxony and his wife, by
Daniel Kellerthaler, inscribed and dated *1608*, height 4⅛in (10.4cm)
London £13,200 ($16,896). 2.IV.85

The medallion was made to commemorate the marriage of the duke in 1607.

A south German gilt-wood relief of the Visitation, circle of Veit Stoss, Nuremberg, *circa* 1500–35,
width 34in (86.4cm)
New York $40,700 (£31,797). 23.XI.84

*Opposite*
A Venetian gilt-wood figure of a saint, from the workshop of Tullio Lombardi, *circa* 1500–1510,
height of figure 40½in (102.9cm)
New York $38,500 (£30,078). 23.XI.84
From the collection of Brown University, Rhode Island

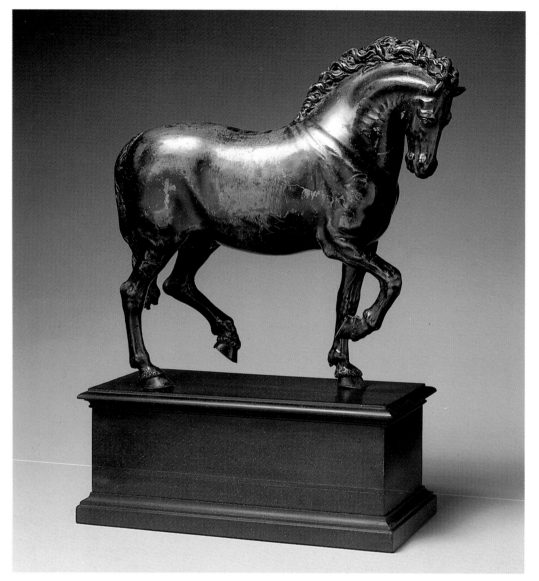

A Florentine bronze study of a stallion, *circa* 1600, height 9⅜in (23.8cm)
London £48,400 ($61,952). 13.XII.84

*Right*
A gilt-bronze figure of St James, seventeenth century,
height 9in (22.9cm)
London £12,100 ($15,488). 2.IV.85

*Left*
A Paduan bronze figure of Venus, attributed to Severo
da Ravenna, *circa* 1500, height 9¾in (24.8cm)
New York $26,400 (£20,625). 23.XI.84

A Florentine bronze group of Hercules and Omphale by Ferdinando Tacca, *circa* 1680,
height 16in (40.7cm)
London £48,400 ($61,952). 2.IV.85

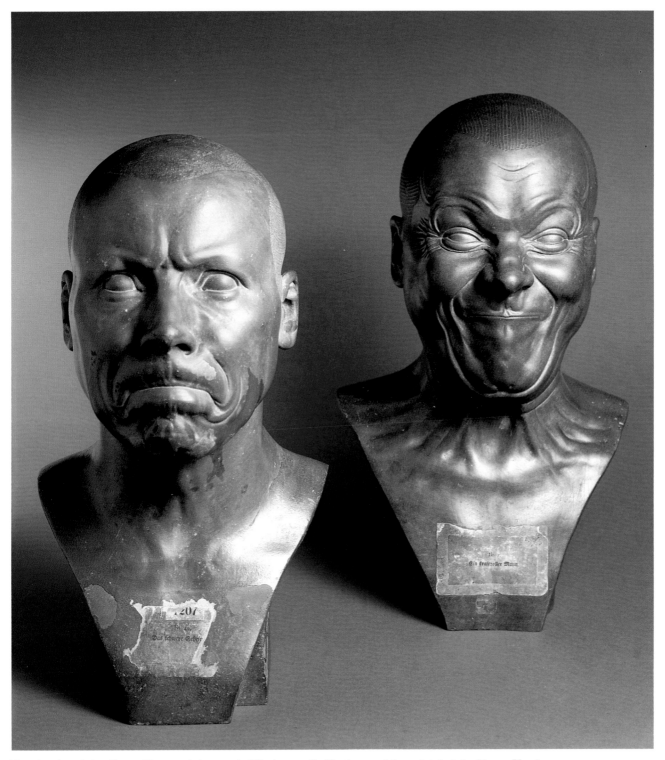

Two lead and tin alloy self-portrait busts, *A difficult secret* (left), *A powerful man* (right), by Franz Xavier
Messerschmidt, *circa* 1770, height 16½in and 16¾in (42cm and 42.6cm)
London £93,500 and £143,000 ($119,680 and $183,040). 2.IV.85

**Matthew Snelling**
A young man, on a prepared
playing card, signed and dated
*Feb 1653* on the reverse,
2½in (6.3cm)
London £8,800 ($11,264).
11.III.85

**Alexander Cooper**
A Dutch nobleman, on vellum,
*circa* 1630, 1¾in (4.5cm)
London £13,750 ($17,600).
11.III.85

**Lorenzo Balbi**
Benedetto, Duke of Chablais,
*circa* 1770, 5⅞in (15cm)
Geneva SFr 41,800
(£12,628:$16,139). 12.XI.84
From the collection of the late
King Umberto II of Italy

**Heinrich Friedrich Füger**
A young lady, signed, *circa* 1785,
2⅜in (6cm)
London £9,020 ($11,546). 19.XI.84

**John Smart**
Mrs George Aubry, signed and
dated *1787 I*, 2¾in (6.8cm)
London £6,380 ($8,166).
19.XI.84

**Jean-Baptiste-Jacques Augustin**
Thomas Weld, later Cardinal Weld and his daughter
Mary Lucy, signed and dated *Paris 1819*, 7in (17.7cm)
London £35,200 ($45,056). 8.VI.85
From the collection of Lord Clifford of Chudleigh, OBE

**Sir William Charles Ross**
A young lady, *circa* 1840, 7⅞in (20cm)
London £6,380 ($8,166). 8.VI.85

A German jewelled four-colour gold snuff box, *circa* 1760, width 3⅜in (8.5cm)
Geneva SFr85,800 (£25,921:$33,127). 16.V.85

The scenes on this box are based on a set of twelve designs by François Boucher, called *Scènes de la Vie Chinoise*, engraved by Huquier.

A German gold and mother-of-pearl snuff box, mid-eighteenth century, width 3⅜in (8.5cm)
Geneva SFr82,500 (£24,924:$31,853). 16.V.85

A gold-mounted *verre eglomisé* snuff box, maker's mark of Adrien-Jean-Maximilien Vachette,
Paris, 1798–1809, width 3⅞in (9.8cm)
Geneva SFr82,500 (£24,924:$31,853). 14.XI.84

A gold-mounted tortoiseshell *piqué* snuff box, maker's mark of Adrien-Jean-Maximilien Vachette,
Paris, 1783–89, width 3⅛in (8cm)
Geneva SFr77,000 (£23,263:$29,730). 14.XI.84

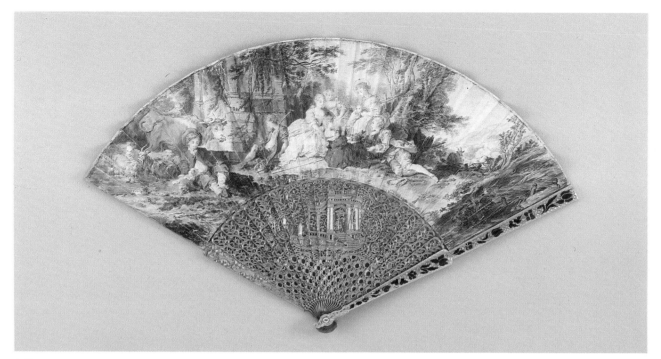

A French gold and enamel fan, second half nineteenth century, length 10½in (26.7cm)
London £7,150 ($9,152). 9.VII.85

An English jewelled, gold and hardstone necessaire,
in the manner of James Cox, *circa* 1765–70,
height 4½in (11.4cm)
Geneva SFr55,000 (£16,616:$21,235). 16.V.85

*Opposite*
A French mother-of-pearl fan, the sticks by Valmour,
signed; painted and signed by A. Soldé, *circa* 1860,
length 11¼in (28.6cm)
London £2,640 ($3,379). 11.III.85

A Swedish gold presentation snuff box, maker's mark of
Frantz Bergs, *circa* 1750, the interior of the lid inset with a
miniature of Lovisa Ulrika, Queen of Sweden,
diameter 3in (7.5cm)
Geneva SFr143,000 (£43,202:$55,212). 16.V.85

This snuff box is traditionally held to have been given
to Charles Irvine of Drum Castle in Aberdeenshire by
Queen Lovisa Ulrika.

# An album of eighteenth-century goldsmiths' designs

## A. Kenneth Snowman

The first stirrings of the creative process are a continuing source of interest and speculation to those who have learned to admire the work of art that emerges from this often tentative groping in the mysterious obscurity of the soul. Sickert curiously called this vital ingredient the 'letch'. How many times have we been enchanted, for example, by an unpretentious Constable sketch only to be let down in front of the final grandiose gallery version of the same scene, in which, too often, a glimpse of nature caught with fleeting tenderness has been quite snuffed out by heavy formal brush-work. A case of stage-fright after a triumphant rehearsal. 'Un petit croquis,' it had been declared, 'vaut mieux que le plus long discours'. A thoroughly sensible remark that we see borne out in the arts again and again.

Among the most beautiful and rewarding messages left to us from the eighteenth century are drawings for snuff boxes. The designers understood exactly the requirements of the craftsmen whose job it was to translate their ideas into reality: the chaser and engraver of gold and silver, the setter of gem-stones and the enameller or lapidary. These jottings, often roughly sketched, were equivalent to the engineer's 'jig', without which he cannot work. Most of the best ideas in the world of fashion emanated from Paris and, indeed, the most original and elegant drawings for snuff boxes and *objets de vertu* generally are Parisian.

The *siècle de la tabatière* really started with the regency of Philippe d'Orléans in 1715 and the dawn of the rococo. The baroque, which had cast a sombre magnificence over the decoration of the great palaces of the Sun King and his court, when adapted and necessarily reduced in scale for the decoration of as small an object as a snuff box, had understandably undergone a great change: a conception based upon grandiosity cannot be successfully miniaturised at will. With what enthusiasm the bright chic of the *régence* must have been welcomed by artists and craftsmen alike, by men such as Oppenord, Meissonnier, Watteau and Cressent, eager to turn their backs on the claustrophobic decoration of the brothers Bérain and face the brilliant light radiated by the rococo. Cyril Connolly has vividly described this revolution in taste as an explosive affirmation of the private life, an escape from Versailles.

The makers of snuff boxes and other small fashionable accessories began to incorporate flowers, birds and insects, shells and rock forms into their designs. To accommodate the new motifs the fundamental design of the box had to be reconsidered and

Fig. 1
One of seven ink and wash designs for snuff box lids, French,
*circa* 1735–60, approximately 2½in by 3⅛in (6.3cm by 8cm)
Geneva SFr2,420 (£731:$934). 14.XI.84
From the collection of the late D. David-Weill

appropriate forms created. At first these were based upon the asymmetrical scrolling of the rococo, as exemplified in the engraved designs by Meissonnier, published in 1725. They inspired the elegant snuff boxes bearing the gallicised name of their maker Daniel Gouers. A box by Gouers is known, similar to a design illustrated (Fig. 1), which is from an album of goldsmiths' designs collected by D. David-Weill and sold in Geneva on 14 November 1984. Such decorative motifs gave way some fifteen to twenty years later to a far simpler abstract and formalised décor. The walls of the rectangular box much favoured at this time, were treated as framed areas of flat-chased or engraved gold, sometimes employing carved mother-of-pearl, stone or lacquer panels, held in cage-work mounts and decorated with enamelled motifs.

The David-Weill album of goldsmiths' designs included, before its dispersal, a particularly beguiling and early example in this format, embellished with various sea-shells, to be carried out in naturalistically coloured enamels (Fig. 2). We are fortunate in this case to be able to trace the actual box that was made in 1742 (Fig. 3) by one of the most distinguished goldsmiths of the eighteenth century, Jean Ducrollay, from this very design, which must presumably be of nearly even date.

Matching a preliminary drawing with a finished box is an intriguing facet of research and an examination of the catalogue of the Geneva sale bears ample testimony to the many successes of John Culme who prepared this section. One of his most notable triumphs, an example of the smooth transition from the artist's drawing

Fig. 2
A watercolour design for a snuff box lid, French, *circa* 1742, 2½in by 3¼in (6.4cm by 8.2cm)
Geneva SFr7,700 (£2,326:$2,973). 14.XI.84
From the collection of the late D. David-Weill

Fig. 4
A pencil and wash design for a snuff box lid, French, *circa* 1756, 3¼in by 4¼in (8.2cm by 10.8cm)
Geneva SFr1,870 (£565:$722). 14.XI.84
From the collection of the late D. David-Weill

Fig. 3
A gold and enamel snuff box, maker's mark of
Jean Ducrollay, Paris, 1742, width 3⅛in (7.8cm)
Private collection

Fig. 5
A gold and diamond snuff box, inscribed by the maker
*L.Roucel à Paris le 29 Juillet 1756* and *Jacqmin joailler du Roi*
for the retailer, Paris, 1756, width 3½in (9cm)
Ajuda Palace, Lisbon
Snowman: *Eighteenth Century Gold Boxes of Europe*

Fig. 6
Two of seven ink and watercolour designs for snuff box lids, French, *circa* 1745–55,
approximately 2½in by 3⅜in (6.4cm by 8.7cm)
Geneva SFr1,980 (£598:$764). 14.XI.84
From the collection of the late D. David-Weill

to an object we know, is to be found in a pencil and wash sketch for the lid of a snuff box to be set with a profusion of large diamonds, some so curious a shape as to prompt the thought that the designer was shown the stones and asked to produce a drawing specifically for them (Fig. 4). The Ajuda Palace in Lisbon includes among its treasures this same rather ungainly gold snuff box, ablaze with just these diamonds (Fig. 5). It was formerly the proud possession of José I of Portugal and is inscribed by the retailer *Jacqmin joailler du Roi* and *L. Roucel à Paris le 29 Juillet 1756* for the maker.

This is an unusual and happy circumstance. Often boxes manifest a distinct affinity with a particular design, but a literal translation from the drawing to an actual artifact is rarely found. There are reasons for this: many fine snuff boxes have simply not survived and another point to be remembered is the way artists worked. A goldsmith, while doubtless inspired by a good design, would always feel free to adapt it to his own or his client's taste, or he may occasionally have been obliged to alter it in the face of unforeseen technical demands. Eugène Delacroix sounded a philosophical note: 'Perhaps the sketch of a work is so pleasing because everyone can finish it as he chooses.'

Some further designs from the early 1740s in the David-Weill album (Fig. 6) showing how the engraver or chaser was to decorate the rectangular gold panel before him, or how the carver of mother-of-pearl was to treat his material, can be related to snuff boxes in both media that approximate to these brown ink and watercolour drawings. The almost machine-like execution of the designs foreshadows a technique subsequently achieved mechanically when, halfway through the century,

Fig. 7
A gold and enamel snuff box, maker's mark of Jacques-Malquis le Quin, Paris, 1749–50,
width 3⅛in (7.9cm)
Reproduced courtesy of the Louvre, Paris

the *tour à guillocher*, or rose engine, was built, providing a method of engraving metal and in large measure supplanting the craft of the hand-engraver. This cheap and quick technique, known as engine-turning, was exploited to the full and within the next fifty years became debased. But upon its first appearance the goldsmiths and silversmiths put the new tool through its paces with great flair and the designers of boxes incorporated new and previously unimagined patterns into their drawings.

Clare Le Corbeiller has quite rightly reminded us that the earliest references to engine-turning in the *Comptes des menus plaisirs*, describing a box '*guillochée à étoiles*' (*sic*) appeared in 1755. But there is solid evidence that the first tentative exercises in the technique were carried out well before this date. One of the most sensational gold snuff boxes in the Louvre, rectangular and decorated on all sides with flowers and birds in polychrome-enamelled relief, against a background of boldly expressed, machine-engraved and irregularly curved reeding, is the work of Jacques-Malquis le Quin and bears the unambiguous Paris date letter for 1749–50 (Fig. 7). The box is illustrated here on account of its almost revolutionary significance: the mechanically drawn loops are, after all, in their wayward asymmetry, an unlikely but true expression of the rococo.

A Fabergé gold, silver and diamond necklace with detachable brooch, workmaster August Holmström, St Petersburg, *circa* 1890
New York $27,500 (£21,484). 11.VI.85

A Fabergé lapis-lazuli, gold, silver and enamel desk clock, workmaster Henrik Wigström, St Petersburg, *circa* 1900, height 2⅝in (6.7cm)
New York $44,000 (£34,375). 11.VI.85

A Fabergé hardstone figure of a carpenter (*plotnik*), workmaster Henrik Wigström, St Petersburg, 1908–1917, height 5in (12.7cm)
London £82,500 ($105,600). 20.II.85

A silver-gilt and shaded enamel *kovsh* in the form of a cockerel, workmaster Pavel Ovchinnikov,
Moscow, 1899–1908, length 11⅜in (29cm)
Geneva SFr55,000 (£16,616:$21,236). 16.V.85

An icon of the Virgin, Moscow, second half sixteenth century, $11\frac{3}{4}$in by $9\frac{7}{8}$in (30cm by 25cm)
London £11,000 ($14,080). 8.XI.84

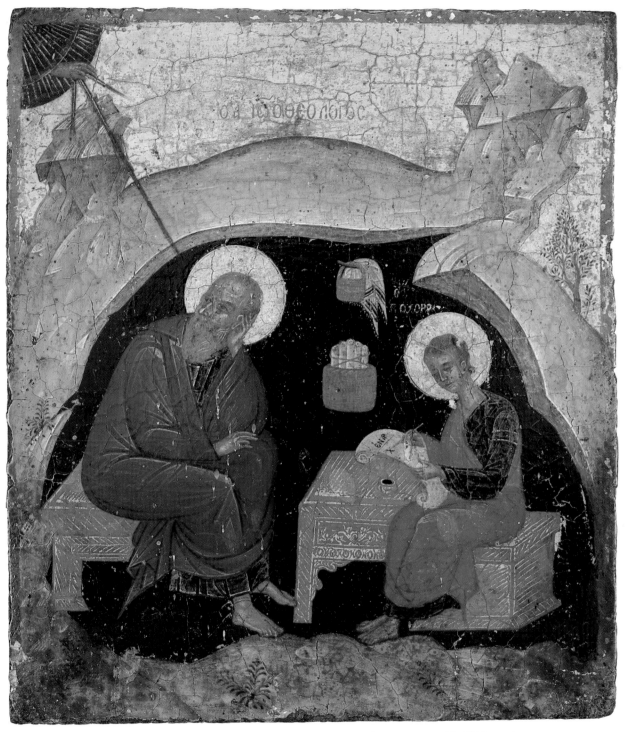

A Cretan icon of St John the Theologian dictating his Gospel to Prokhoros, second half fifteenth century, 10¼in by 9in (26cm by 23cm)
London £9,350 ($11,968). 20.II.85

# Clocks
# and watches

An enamel plaque depicting the Judgement of Paris by Pierre Huaud, signed, seventeenth century, 3⅜in by 2⅝in (8.5cm by 6.7cm) Geneva SFr 35,200 (£10,634 : $13,591). 13.XI.84

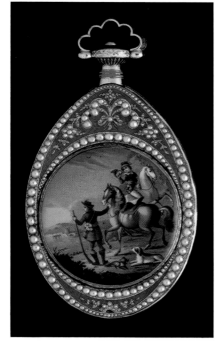

A gold, enamel and pearl cased sweep-seconds watch for the Oriental market, *circa* 1800, length 4in (10.2cm) New York $63,250 (£49,414). 24.X.84

A gold and enamel verge watch by Les Deux Frères Huaut Les Jeunes, Geneva, *circa* 1720, the movement by Jan Bernardus Vrythoff, The Hague, diameter 1⅝in (4.2cm) New York $56,100 (£43,828). 17.VI.85

**John Kenebel No. 540**
A gold, enamel and pearl cased sweep-seconds watch for the Oriental market, London, 1799, length 3¾in (9.5cm) New York $25,300 (£19,766). 17.VI.85

A silver pair cased wandering-hour verge
watch by S. Bastien Mestral, Paris, early
eighteenth century, diameter 2⅝in (6.5cm)
Geneva SFr 24,200 (£7,311:$9,344).
13.XI.84

**Charles Frodsham No. 09364**
A gold open face keyless lever
one-minute tourbillon, London, 1910,
diameter 2⅝in (6.5cm)
Geneva SFr 66,000 (£19,940:$25,483).
13.XI.84

**Josiah Emery No. 873**
A gold cased lever watch, London, 1781,
diameter 2¼in (5.6cm)
London £26,400 ($33,792). 28.II.85
This is the earliest datable Emery lever watch.

A gold and enamel hunting cased minute-repeating
fusee keyless lever *grand sonnerie* clockwatch with
chronograph, perpetual calendar and moon phases,
for the Mexican market by Esmeralda, Mexico and
Paris, *circa* 1894
New York $55,000 (£42,969). 24.X.84

*Above, top row, left to right*

A gold wristwatch by Vacheron & Constantin, 1957, diameter 1⅜in (3.5cm), £1,265 ($1,619)

A gold wristwatch by Rolex, 1928, length 1½in (3.8cm), £880 ($1,126)

A gold wristwatch by Cartier, length 1⅛in (3cm), £2,750 ($3,520)

A gold wristwatch by Patek Philippe, No. 834704, length 1⅜in (3.6cm), £1,870 ($2,394)

A gold perpetual calendar wristwatch by Patek Philippe, No. 967642, *circa* 1950–52, diameter 1⅜in (3.4cm), £9,900 ($12,672)

*Below, lower row, left to right*

A gold Oyster day-date centre seconds wristwatch by Rolex, diameter 1⅜in (3.4cm), £3,850 ($4,928)

A gold wristwatch by Autorist, 1931, length 1⅝in (4cm), £715 ($915)

A gold, diamond and sapphire wristwatch by Cartier, length 1⅛in (2.8cm), £3,190 ($4,083)

A gold wristwatch by Patek Philippe, No. 832412, 1937, length 1¾in (4.4cm), £2,090 ($2,675)

A gold Seamaster wristwatch by Omega, stamped *Apollo XI 1969, First Watch Worn on the Moon*, diameter 1½in (3.9cm), £1,870 ($2,394)

The above wristwatches were sold in London on 28 February 1985

A gold self-winding water-resistant perpetual calendar wristwatch by Patek Philippe & Co. No. 119686, diameter 1½in (3.8cm) New York $15,400 (£12,031). 24.X.84

**George Graham No. 657**
A walnut longcase clock, London,
*circa* 1725, height 7ft 6in (229.5cm)
London £19,800 ($25,344). 1.XI.84
From the collection of C. Myers, Esq.

An astronomical calendar clock, signed *John Naylor*, height 38in (96.5cm)
London £42,900 ($54,912). 28.II.85
From the collection of Lt-Col John Cookson, DSO, DL

An engraving with the date *March the first 1725/6*, depicting the dial of this (or a nearly identical) clock and giving a detailed account of its functions, was sold at the same time. The signature on the engraving reads *Jon. Naylor near Namptwich Cheshire*, but the clock was probably made in London, or at least for a London customer, as instructions are given for calculating the time of high tide at London Bridge. After leaving Cheshire Naylor worked in King Street, Covent Garden; he died in 1752.

A silvered metal quarter-repeating musical automaton clock for the Oriental market by
William Carpenter, London, 1780, height 38in (96.5cm)
Geneva SFr154,000 (£46,526:$59,459). 13.XI.84

# Musical instruments

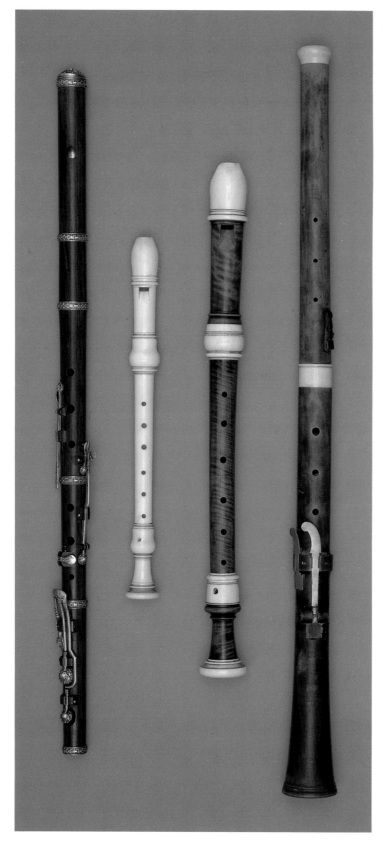

*Left to right*
An eight-keyed cocuswood flute by Rudall &
Rose, London, *circa* 1830, stamped *Rudall & Rose,*
*No. 15, Piazza, Covent Garden, London, 594,*
sounding length 23in (58.4cm)
London £2,310 ($2,957). 3.IV.85

An ivory descant (soprano) recorder, continental,
early eighteenth century, length 13⅞in (35.2cm)
London £3,960 ($5,069). 3.IV.85

A stained boxwood treble (alto) recorder
by Urquhart, stamped *Urquhart,* early
eighteenth century, length 19⅝in (49.9cm)
London £3,520 ($4,506). 3.IV.85

A two-keyed stained pearwood tenor oboe by
William Milhouse, Newark, stamped *Milhouse,*
*Newark, circa* 1775, length 28 9/16 in (72.6cm)
London £1,980 ($2,534). 3.IV.85

*Opposite*
A chamber organ by England & Son, London,
1790, inscribed *England & Son, Londini fecit 1790,*
*Stephen Street, Tottenham Court Road,*
height 10ft 3⅜in (313.5cm)
London £20,900 ($26,752). 22.XI.84
From the collection of Major and
Mrs T. Bagshawe

The 'Cathédrale' violin by Antonio Stradivari, Cremona, 1707, labelled *Antonius Stradiuarius Cremonensis Faciebat 1707*, length of back 14in (35.6cm)
London £396,000 ($506,880). 22.XI.84

The 'Jules Falk' violin by Antonio Stradivari,
Cremona, 1723, labelled *Antonius Stradiuarius
Cremonensis Faciebat Anno 1723,*
length of back 14⅛in (35.9cm)
London £286,000 ($366,080). 3.IV.85

The 'Rosenheim' violin by Antonio Stradivari,
Cremona, 1686, labelled *Antonins Stradiuarius
Cremonensis Faciebat Anno 1686,*
length of back 14 1/16 in (35.7cm)
London £165,000 ($211,200). 22.XI.84

A violoncello by Jean-Baptiste Vuillaume, Paris,
labelled *Jean Baptiste Vuillaume a Paris / Rue Croix des
Petit Champs*, length of back 29⅝in (75.2cm)
New York $40,700 (£31,797). 19.VI.85

A violoncello by Peter Guarneri of Venice, 1725,
labelled *Petrus Guarnerius Cremonensis Filii Josef Fecit
Venetis Anno 1725*, length of back 29½in (74.9cm)
London £148,500 ($190,080). 3.IV.85

A violin by Tommaso Balestrieri, Mantua, 1771, labelled *Thomas Balestrieri Cremonensis / Fecit Mantuae Anno 1771*, length of back 13⅞in (35.2cm) New York $47,300 (£36,953). 19.VI.85

A violin by Joannes Baptista Guadagnini, Turin, 1773, labelled *Jo: Bap: Guadagnini Cremonen: fecit / Taurini directione D I A Cotii / Typis Antonii Stradivari 1773*, length of back 13¹³⁄₁₆in (35.1cm) New York $115,500 (£90,234). 19.VI.85 From the collection of the late Yoko Matsuo Levitch

# Furniture and tapestries

One of a pair of George I walnut-veneered chairs, *circa* 1720
London £48,400 ($61,952). 8.III.85

A George III sycamore, mahogany and satinwood marquetry bow-front secretaire bookcase,
last quarter eighteenth century, height 8ft 1in (246.5cm)
New York $101,750 (£79,492). 26.I.85

Two of a set of twelve George III mahogany armchairs by Gillows of Lancaster, 1789–90
New York $176,000 (£137,500). 13.IV.85
From the collection of Mr and Mrs Edwin H. Herzog

One of a pair of George II gilt-wood benches, mid-eighteenth century, length 5ft 3in (160cm)
New York $48,400 (£37,813). 26.I.85
From the collection of the Fine Arts Committee of the United States Department of State

A George III mahogany and marble-inlaid side table, last quarter eighteenth century,
width 5ft (152.5cm)
New York $42,900 (£33,516). 13.IV.85
From the collection of Mr and Mrs Edwin H. Herzog

One of a pair of George III japanned chinoiserie display cabinets-on-stands, *circa* 1760,
height 6ft 7in (201cm)
London £61,600 ($78,848). 8.III.85
From the collection of the late Sir Michael Duff, Bt

A Regency parcel-gilt black lacquer penwork cabinet, first quarter nineteenth century,
height 4ft 8in (142.2cm)
New York $36,300 (£28,359). 16.XI.84
From the collection of the late Pauline K. Cave

A rosewood, ebony, mother-of-pearl and glass mechanical writing desk with gilt-bronze-mounted ivory columns, designed by C.E. Davis *circa* 1863, made by Thomas Knight, with Royal Worcester panels designed by Arthur Murch and made by Thomas Bott, width 4ft 7⅛in (140cm) London £31,900 ($40,832). 22.II.85

The desk was presented by the people of Bath in 1870 to Princess Alexandra of Denmark to celebrate her marriage to the Prince of Wales. Thomas Bott, who produced the porcelain plaques depicting episodes from British history, was frequently patronised by Queen Victoria.

A Louis XV gilt-bronze-mounted lacquer commode, stamped *B.V.R.B.*, mid-eighteenth century, width 4ft ½in (123.2cm)
New York $352,000 (£275,000). 4.V.85

Bernard van Risamburgh was received Master during the reign of Louis XV.

*Opposite, above*
Two of a set of four Louis XV caned beechwood *fauteuils à la reine, circa* 1730
New York $129,250 (£100,977). 4.V.85

*Opposite, below*
A pair of Louis XIV gilt-bronze chenets, attributed to André-Charles Boulle, last quarter seventeenth century, height 13in (33cm)
New York $55,000 (£42,969). 4.V.85

A Louis XV gilt-bronze-mounted *bois satiné*, kingwood and fruitwood marquetry cartonnier, stamped with the mark of Pierre II Migeon, mid-eighteenth century, height 7ft 1½in (217cm)
New York $286,000 (£223,438). 17.XI.84

Pierre II Migeon was received Master *circa* 1738

A central German alabaster-veneered writing cabinet, *circa* 1730, height 5ft 3in (160cm)
London £49,500 ($63,360). 24.V.85

A Louis XV gilt-bronze-mounted boulle marquetry
clock and pedestal, attributed to Jean-Pierre Latz,
*circa* 1740, height 8ft 6in (259cm)
New York $275,000 (£214,844). 17.XI.84

*Opposite*
A Venetian *lacca povera* bureau cabinet, *circa* 1740,
height 8ft 7½in (263cm)
London £220,000 ($281,600). 30.XI.84

The cartouche on the cornice suggests that this
cabinet was made for a Pope.

A Louis XIV Savonnerie carpet, *circa* 1667–89, 11ft 2in by 10ft 7in (340cm by 323cm)
London £104,500 ($133,760). 30.XI.84

One of a set of four Louis XV gilt-wood armchairs stamped *G.Avisse*
Monte Carlo FF 1,332,000 (£111,000:$142,156). 23.VI.85

Guillaume Avisse was received Master in 1743.

One of a pair of gilt-bronze-mounted, hardstone and ebony pier cabinets, first quarter
nineteenth century, height 3ft 4½in (103cm)
London £143,000 ($183,040). 30.XI.84

These cabinets are believed to have belonged to William Beckford and bear the cinquefoil device that
he favoured.

A Sèvres porcelain and gilt-bronze-mounted *bois de citron* guéridon,
stamped *M. Carlin*, the Sèvres plaque marked with date letter *X* in blue for 1775,
height 2ft 10¼in (87cm)
Monte Carlo FF 1,443,000 (£120,250:$154,002). 23.VI.85

Martin Carlin was received Master in 1766.

A Beauvais tapestry, *L'île de Cythère* or *Le temple de Vénus*, by Jacques Duplessis, signed and dated *1725*,
13ft 7in by 14ft 5in (415cm by 440cm)
Monte Carlo FF 399,600 (£33,300:$42,647). 24.VI.85

*Opposite*
A Franco-Flemish millefleurs tapestry, possibly Tournai, *circa* 1500–25,
11ft 2in by 8ft 4in (340cm by 254cm)
New York $220,000 (£171,875). 11.V.85
From the collection of the late Colonel C. Michael Paul

# Silver

A chinoiserie chocolate cup and cover, maker's mark of Ralph Leake, London, *circa* 1685,
height 4⅞in (12.5cm)
London £44,000 ($56,320). 23.V.85

A set of four Charles II candlesticks, maker's mark of Jacob Bodendick, London, 1677,
height 10¼in (26cm)
New York $203,500 (£158,984). 13.XII.84
From the collection of the Fine Arts Committee of the United States Department of State

A George II wine cistern, maker's mark of Thomas Folkingham, London, *circa* 1728–29,
width 23⅝in (60cm)
New York $275,000 (£214,844). 26.IV.85

A pair of George II candlesticks, maker's mark of Lewis Pantin, London, 1734, height 11⅜in (29cm)
London £39,600 ($50,688). 23.V.85

The candlesticks, which bear the arms of Sir Watkin Williams Wynn, are early examples of cast and
chased English rococo silver.

A George II dinner service, known as the Thanet dinner service, 110 pieces, maker's mark of Paul de Lamerie, London, 1742–46
London £825,000 ($1,056,000). 22.XI.84
From the collection of the late Baron Hothfield

This dinner service was commissioned by the wealthy politician and classical scholar Sackville Tufton, 7th Earl of Thanet. He married Lady Mary Saville, heiress of the Marquess of Halifax in 1722. The marriage was not a happy one and in 1747 the Countess of Thanet set up a separate establishment across the square from her husband, at 44 Grosvenor Square, where she scandalised society, behaving 'without any regard to public censure.' She died on 30 July 1751, two days before Paul de Lamerie, who was 'much regretted by his Family and Acquaintance as a Tender Father, a Kind Master and an upright Dealer'.

One of a set of four George III wine coolers in the style of Paul de Lamerie, maker's mark of Paul
Storr for Storr & Co., for Rundell, Bridge & Rundell, London, 1817–18, height 11in (28cm)
London £121,000 ($154,880). 22.XI.84
From the collection of Lord Binning

A pair of George IV sauce boats, maker's mark of Paul Storr for Storr & Mortimer, London, 1823, length 10in (25.5cm)
London £35,200 ($45,056). 23.V.85

A George III silver-gilt wine cooler, maker's mark of Paul Storr for Storr & Co., for Rundell, Bridge & Rundell, London, 1814, height 10⅝in (27cm)
London £21,450 ($27,456). 23.V.85

This wine cooler appears to be an unrecorded version of an example of 1817–18, also Storr & Co., for Rundell, Bridge & Rundell, in the collection of the Duke of Wellington. Apart from the figurework, the general form and decoration of this cooler is close to that of Flaxman's Theocritus Cup of *circa* 1809 and may, indeed, have been intended as its companion.

A nautilus shell cup with enamelled and ruby-set silver-gilt mounts, attributed to
Johann Heinrich Köhler of Dresden, *circa* 1720, height 11¾in (29.8cm)
Geneva SFr 132,000 (£39,879 : $50,965). 14.XI.84

The quality of this cup and the lack of hallmarks indicate that it was made for a
royal patron, while the combination of materials suggests the court of Saxony. The
unusual carving of the helm in the inside of the shell, and the silver-gilt dragon are
remarkably similar to those of another seventeenth-century cup mounted by the
Dresden court jeweller Johann Heinrich Köhler in the 1720s.

A ewer and basin, bearing the arms of Milan, maker's mark of Giovanni Bellezza, signed and dated,
Milan, 1847, diameter of basin 25⅞in (65.8cm); height of ewer 27⅜in (69.5cm)
Geneva SFr 374,000 (£112,991 : $144,402). 14.XI.84

*Opposite, above*
A silver-gilt service, comprising tea pot, chocolate pot, sugar box and slop bowl, maker's mark of
Johann Ludwig Biller II, Augsburg, 1735–36, height of chocolate pot 10½in (26.7cm)
Geneva SFr 231,000 (£69,789 : $89,189). 14.V.85

*Opposite, below*
A silver-gilt ecuelle with cover and stand, maker's mark of Jean-Louis Imlin III, Strasbourg,
*circa* 1750, width 11⅞in (30.2cm)
Geneva SFr 68,200 (£20,604 : $26,332). 14.V.85

# European ceramics and glass

A pair of Meissen figures of *The thrown kiss*, modelled by Johann Joachim Kaendler, *circa* 1737, height 5⅝in (14.4cm)
New York $26,400 (£20,625). 21.V.85
From the collection of Jack and Belle Linsky

These figures, modelled from the engraving *Le baiser rendu* by Pierre Filloeul after the painting by Jean-Baptiste-Joseph Pater, were described by Kaendler in an entry in his workbook for December 1736.

A Meissen group of two parrots, modelled by Johann Joachim Kaendler, *circa* 1744,
height 14¼in (36.1cm)
New York $56,100 (£43,828). 4.V.85
From the collection of Henry Ford II

A Meissen chinoiserie arbour figure modelled by Johann Joachim Kaendler, 1734,
height 9¾in (24.8cm)
London £25,300 ($32,384). 25.VI.85

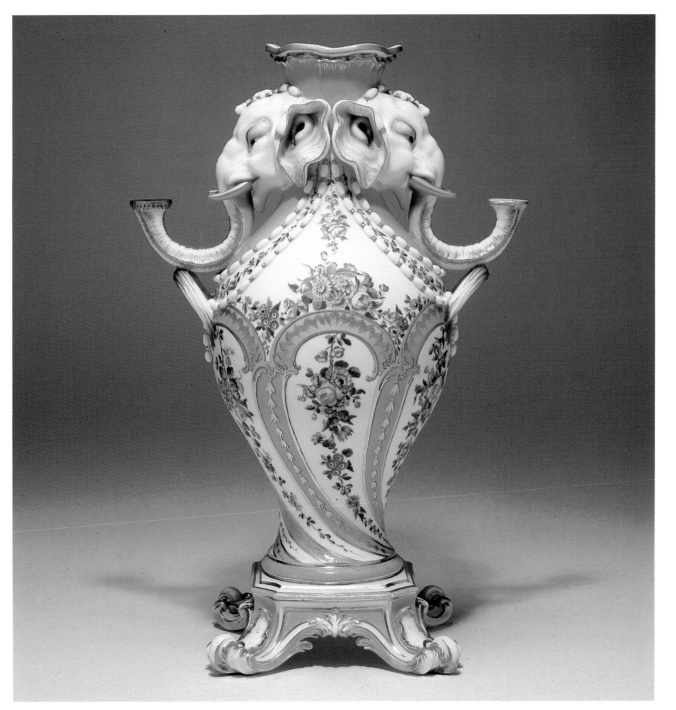

A Sèvres *rose pompadour* elephant vase, modelled by Jean-Claude Duplessis, père, marked with
interlaced *L*s and date letter *E* in blue enamel for 1757, height 15⅜in (39cm)
New York $115,500 (£90,234). 17.XI.84
From the collection of Mrs Charles Wrightsman

The elephants' heads were probably inspired by Meissen versions of Chinese designs, modelled by
Johann Joachim Kaendler.

A pair of silver-gilt-mounted Sèvres *vases à glace* decorated with views of European palaces painted by Jean-François Robert, each signed and marked with crowned eagle, *circa* 1814, height 13⅝in (34.6cm) New York $110,000 (£85,938). 17.XI.84

The vases once formed part of the *Service à vues diverses* ordered by Napoleon I in 1812. Production at the Imperial porcelain manufactory was curtailed at the fall of the First Empire, when the Sèvres factory was occupied by Prussian officers in 1815. The service was completed in 1817, during the reign of Louis XVIII.

*Opposite*
A Berlin vase decorated with a view of the city after Eduard Gaertner, *circa* 1833, height 20½in (52cm) London £19,800 ($25,344). 9.X.84

A Vincennes sugar bowl and cover, marked with interlaced *L*s in blue, *circa* 1750, height 4⅜in (11cm)
London £9,900 ($12,672). 5.III.85

A Vincennes dish, marked with interlaced *L*s in blue, *circa* 1752, diameter 9½in (24cm)
London £3,960 ($5,069). 5.III.85

*Left to right*
A Worcester yellow-ground bowl, *circa* 1770, diameter 9in (23cm)
London £5,720 ($7,322). 21.V.85
From the S.H.V. Hickson Collection

A Worcester plate, painted after a Sèvres original in the atelier of James Giles, *circa* 1770, diameter 8¾in (22.4cm)
London £2,640 ($3,379). 21.V.85
From the S.H.V. Hickson Collection

A Creussen stoneware *krause*, inscribed *IOHANNES, WILHELM, RIHM, 1671,*
height 6¼in (16cm)
London £7,700 ($9,856). 5.III.85

*Opposite*
A pair of Minton 'majolica' blackamoors, 1870, height 70⅝in (179.5cm)
London £52,800 ($67,584). 26.II.85

The designs for these figures were based on a pair of gilt-bronze candelabra
modelled by Carrier de Belleuse for M. Denière, Paris, which in turn had been
taken from designs by Jean le Pautre (1617–82).

A commemorative bowl, enamelled in the Beilby atelier, *circa* 1765, diameter 9½in (24cm)
London £19,800 ($25,344). 12.XI.84
From the collection of Squadron Leader James Rush

The Beilbys, Ralph, William and Mary, were a family of glass painters from Newcastle upon Tyne.

A Mount Washington magnum
rose weight,
diameter 4⅛in (10.5cm)
New York $22,000 (£17,188).
1.XI.84

A Baccarat flat-bouquet weight,
diameter 3in (7.7cm)
London £7,700 ($9,850).
1.VII.85

A Clichy pedestal weight,
diameter of foot 2⅞in (7.4cm)
London £12,650 ($16,192).
1.VII.85

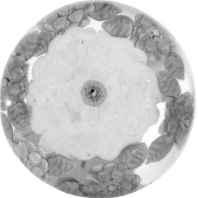

A Clichy flower weight,
diameter 2⅞in (7.3cm)
New York $11,000 (£8,594).
1.XI.84

A Clichy camelia weight,
diameter 3⅛in (8cm)
New York $8,250 (£6,445).
1.XI.84

# American furniture
# and decorative arts

The Williams Family Queen Anne mahogany tray-top tea table, Boston, Massachusetts,
*circa* 1740–60, width 29¾in (75.5cm)
New York $253,000 (£197,656). 8.XII.84
From the collection of Edward S. Williams

A Chippendale mahogany wing armchair, Philadelphia, *circa* 1770
New York $88,000 (£68,750). 8.XII.84

A Chippendale mahogany secretary-bookcase, Goddard-Townsend school, Newport,
Rhode Island, *circa* 1765, height 6ft 11in (211cm)
New York $52,250 (£40,820). 8.XII.84

The Loockerman Family Chippendale mahogany highboy, attributed to Thomas Affleck,
Philadelphia, *circa* 1770, height 8ft 10in (269.4cm)
New York $308,000 (£240,625). 2.II.85

A Federal mahogany card table inlaid with ebony and satinwood, eastern Massachusetts, *circa* 1795, width 36in (91.5cm)
New York $115,500 (£90,234). 1.II.85
From the collection of Abram R. and Blanche M. Harpending

The Van Rensselaer pair of classical mahogany barrel-back armchairs, attributed to Duncan Phyfe,
New York, *circa* 1830
New York $104,500 (£81,641). 1.II.85
From the collection of the late Berry B. Tracy

A Federal mahogany miniature longcase clock,
New Jersey, *circa* 1800, height 4ft 2½in (128.3cm)
New York $154,000 (£120,313). 1.II.85
From the collection of Abram R. and
Blanche M. Harpending

A Federal gilt-bronze-mounted mahogany lighthouse
clock by Simon Willard, Roxbury, Massachusetts,
*circa* 1825, height 2ft 1in (63.5cm)
New York $286,000 (£223,438). 2.II.85
From the collection of the late Winthrop L. Carter

*Left*
A teapot, maker's mark of Joseph Dubois, New York, *circa* 1795, height 6½in (16.5cm)
New York $3,300 (£2,578). 31.I.85
*Centre*
A teapot, maker's mark of John David, Philadelphia, *circa* 1785, height 6¼in (15.9cm)
New York $9,350 (£7,305). 31.I.85
*Right*
A sugar urn and cover, maker's mark of Joseph and Nathaniel Richardson, Philadelphia, *circa* 1785,
height 8½in (21.6cm)
New York $6,050 (£4,727). 31.I.85

A pieced, appliquéd and trapunto album quilt, Baltimore, *circa* 1840,
108in by 104in (274.5cm by 264.3cm)
New York $17,600 (£13,750). 8.XII.84

A gilt-copper weathervane of a Massasoit Indian by Harris & Co., Boston, late nineteenth century, height 38in (96.5cm)
New York $34,100 (£26,641). 28.VI.85

# Nineteenth-century decorative arts

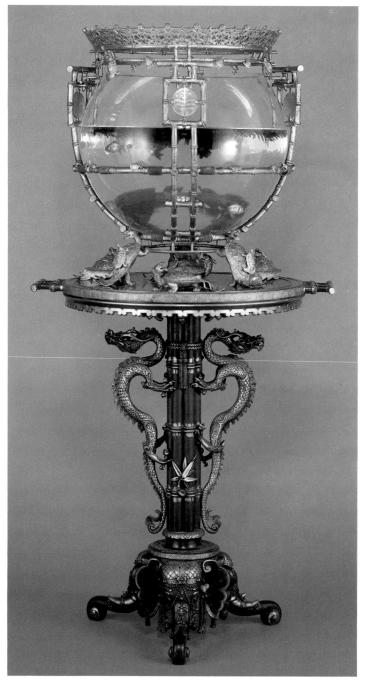

*Opposite*
A gilt-bronze and champlevé enamel three-piece
chinoiserie clock garniture, for Tiffany and Co.,
Paris, last quarter nineteenth century,
height of clock $33\frac{1}{4}$in (84.5cm)
New York $33,000 (£25,781). 15.XII.84

A gilt-bronze-mounted lacquer and kingwood
commode by Bontemps, signed, Paris,
late nineteenth century, width 5ft (152.5cm)
New York $18,700 (£14,609). 15.XII.84

*Left*
A parcel-gilt bronze chinoiserie fish bowl and stand
by Ferdinand Barbedienne, signed, Paris, *circa* 1880,
height 4ft $10\frac{1}{4}$in (148cm)
New York $22,000 (£17,188). 30.III.85

A gilt-bronze-mounted chinoiserie and kingwood secretaire cabinet, stamped *Beurdeley*, Paris, *circa* 1860, height 5ft (152.5cm)
London £19,800 ($25,344). 9.XI.84

An ebony and lacquer *bonheur du jour*, stamped *G.Durand*, Paris, *circa* 1860, height 3ft 10in (117cm)
London £20,900 ($26,752). 9.XI.84

A parcel-gilt bronze group of *Hunting in the Sahara* by Alfred Dubucand, signed, *circa* 1875,
height 31⅛in (79cm)
London £26,400 ($33,792). 21.III.85

*Opposite, above*
A pair of gilt-bronze-mounted green marble fifteen-light candelabra, Paris, mid-nineteenth century,
height 39in (99cm)
London £20,350 ($26,048). 22.III.85

*Opposite, below*
A pair of bronze studies of a *Turkish horse* by Antoine-Louis Barye, signed, *circa* 1840,
heights 11½in and 11¼in (29.2cm and 28.5cm)
London £52,800 ($67,584). 27.XI.84

A bronze figure of *Perseus with the head of Medusa*
by Frederick William Pomeroy, signed and dated *1898*,
height 20 in (51cm)
London £15,950 ($20,416). 13.XII.84

A bronze figure of *An Eton boy* by Bertram MacKennal,
signed, *circa* 1923, height 74in (188cm)
London £51,700 ($66,176). 13.XII.84

A bronze and enamel figure of *Sigurd* by Gilbert Bayes, signed, *circa* 1909, height 28in (71cm)
London £63,800 ($81,664). 12.IV.85

# Art Nouveau
# and Art Deco

A Guild of Handicraft Ltd oak cabinet with ivory inlay, designed by Charles Robert Ashbee,
*circa* 1906–1907, height 4ft 7½in (141cm)
London £52,800 ($67,584). 2.V.85

The cabinet was sold with Ashbee's watercolour design, dated *31–12–06*.

A Martin Brothers stoneware owl, dated *1893*, height 26$\frac{7}{8}$in (68.4cm)
London £47,300 ($60,544). 3.V.85

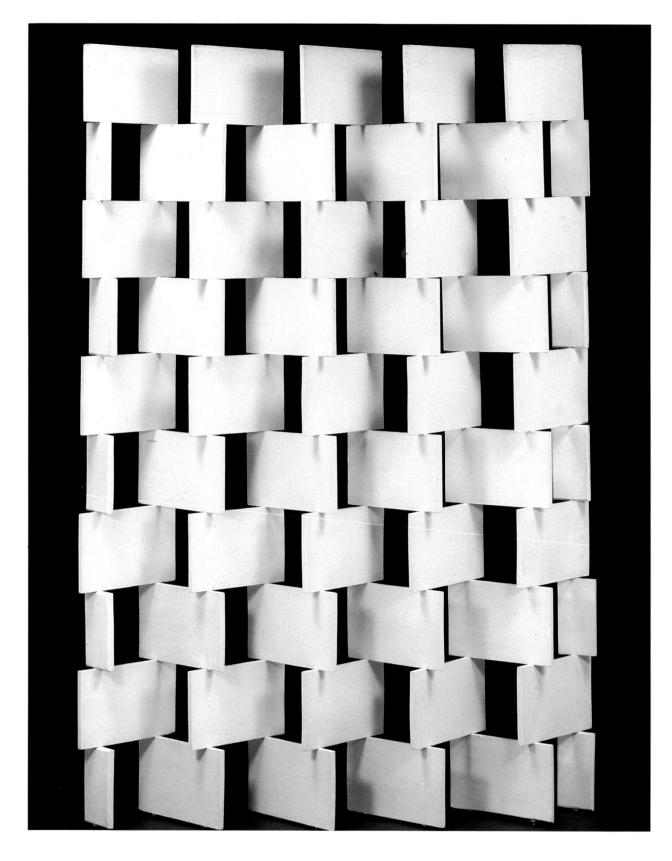

An iron and wood desk with pivoting tray designed by Pierre Chareau, *circa* 1930,
width 4ft 2⅜in (128cm)
Monte Carlo FF 555,000 (£46,250: $59,232). 17.III.85

*Opposite*
A painted wood screen by Eileen Gray, *circa* 1923, height 6ft 11in (211cm)
Monte Carlo FF 444,000 (£37,000: $47,385). 7.X.84

A Morris & Co. embroidered three-fold screen, *circa* 1889, each panel 4ft 8⅛in by 2ft ⅜in
(142.5cm by 62cm)
London £18,700 ($23,936). 29.XI.84

The screen was made as part of the commission to decorate Bullerswood in Kent, home of the
Sanderson family, who were friends of William Morris. The panels were probably designed by
May Morris.

A fruitwood and parquetry grand piano by Louis Majorelle, *circa* 1900, length 6ft 5in (195.7cm)
New York $30,800 (£24,063). 18.V.85

An ebonised wood armchair designed by Paul Iribe, *circa* 1913
New York $18,700 (£14,609). 23.II.85

*Opposite, left*
A Daum glass and gilt-bronze floor lamp by Edgar Brandt, *circa* 1925, height 5ft 5½in (166.5cm)
New York $37,400 (£29,219). 23.II.85

*Opposite, right*
A Tiffany Favrile glass and bronze floor lamp, 1899–1920, height 7ft (213.5cm)
New York $176,000 (£137,500). 17.XI.84

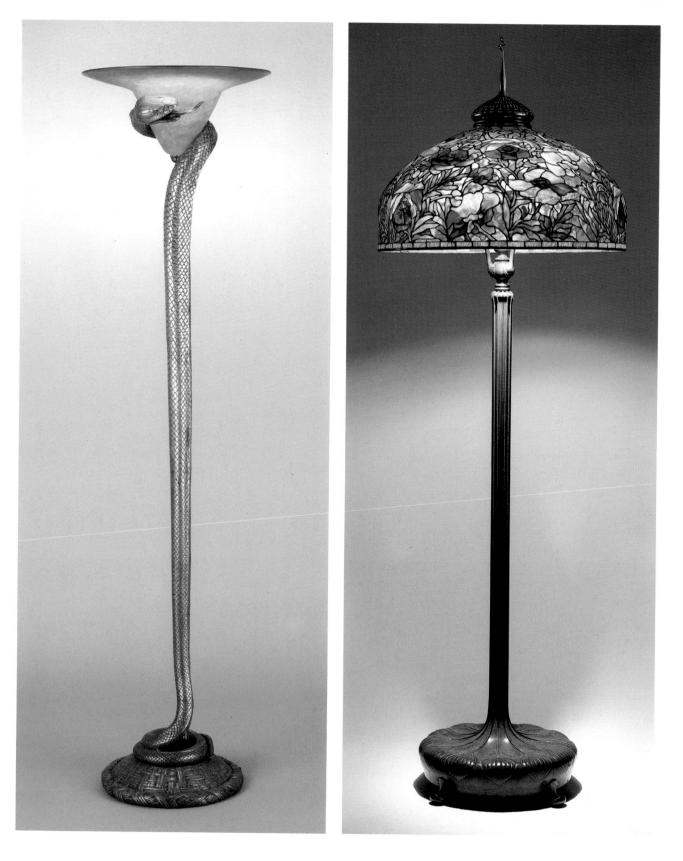

# A cabinet by Koloman Moser

Philippe Garner

The highlight of a sale of twentieth-century decorative arts in Monte Carlo on 7 October 1984 was a slender cabinet designed by the distinguished Viennese artist Koloman Moser (Fig. 1). When Sotheby's were consulted on the sale of this piece, research revealed that a three-legged corner version of otherwise identical design had been presented in 1900 at the eighth Exhibition of the Vienna Secession.

With the doors closed, the only decoration on the cabinet consists of a large circular silvered copper lock-plate *repoussé* with a curious mask, applied iridescent glass teardrops and a restrained frieze top and bottom of stylised flowers, with undulating lines in dark wood, applied in low relief. When opened, however, the cabinet reveals a more decorative interior, the two doors and a pivoting centre panel becoming a triptych, each inlaid in metal and woods, with a mysterious crowned figure of a young woman.

The piece is fascinating for a variety of reasons, expressing, as it does, the aesthetic concerns of the avant-garde design movement in Vienna at a crucial stage of its evolution and, of course, giving a rare opportunity to appreciate the potential of one of the most gifted and influential figures within the Vienna group. Moser and his colleagues are well known for the stylish yet less ambitious furniture that they designed for series production by such firms as Thonet or J. & J. Köhn. Exhibition pieces or private commissions allowed them greater freedom and the possibility of a higher standard of craftsmanship, introducing more complex decoration. Few such pieces survive and the study of examples such as this cabinet, or the richly inlaid desk by Moser sold in Monte Carlo in April 1982 (Fig. 2), serve to extend our understanding of the Secessionist movement's ideals and achievements.

The Vienna Secession was the title adopted by a group of artists and designers who rallied together in the late 1890s, united by their dissatisfaction with the artistic establishment and determined to evolve a new aesthetic based on the rejection of historicism. The group had its counterparts in Great Britain, Germany, France and Belgium, in the movements that developed from the teachings of John Ruskin and William Morris and in the flowering of the curvilinear Art Nouveau style. Numerous

A rosewood cabinet inlaid with coloured woods and metals, designed by Koloman Moser, Vienna, 1900, height 5ft 7⅞in (172.5cm)
Monte Carlo FF 2,331,000 (£194,250 : $248,773). 7.X.84

art journals were published, on the model of the British *The Studio*, founded in 1893, and served to disseminate new ideas and styles. The Viennese avant-garde founded the Association of Austrian Visual Artists in 1897 and this group, which included Otto Wagner, Josef Olbrich, Josef Hoffmann, Koloman Moser and Gustav Klimt, formed themselves into an exhibition society, inaugurating their Secessionist Exhibition Gallery in 1898. That year also saw the first appearance of the journal *Ver Sacrum*, illustrating and promoting the work of the Secessionists.

The pages of *Ver Sacrum* confirm the extent to which the Viennese group shared common roots with Art Nouveau in this first phase of their activity. The influences of Japanese art, of symbolist literature and of nature are much in evidence. The eighth Secessionist exhibition in 1900, in which the three-legged version of the present cabinet was featured, marked a crucial stage in the evolution of the Vienna style.

The Secessionists had invited the Scottish architect–designer Charles Rennie Mackintosh to exhibit alongside them. The restrained dignity of his work, with its emphasis on the rectilinear, its sophisticated rigour of line and decoration, had a considerable impact on the Viennese and became the major influence on the second phase of the Secessionists' work. In 1903 Hoffman and Moser founded the Wiener Werkstätte, a craft co-operative on the model of the Guild of Handicraft formed by Charles Robert Ashbee in Britain. Their work from 1900 till around 1906, the year of Moser's departure from the Werkstätte, is characterised by a rigid geometry of form and decoration, often incorporating the chequer motif so dear to Mackintosh.

Moser's 1900 cabinets mark a turning point, encapsulating the ingredients of the first phase of the Vienna Secessionist style. The formalised flowers and symbolist figures call to mind the elegant stylisation of Japanese graphics and such contemporary counterparts as the two-dimensional inventions of Alphonse Mucha, Georges de Feure, Will Bradley or Jan Toorop. Only the simple rectangular form of the cabinet structure seems to prophesy the path that Moser and his colleagues were to follow. It makes an interesting comparison with the desk designed by Moser in 1902 (Fig. 2). Richly decorated with a geometric repeat pattern inlaid in marquetry, it contrasts with the flowing lines of the cabinet triptych.

The influence of Charles Rennie Mackintosh on the Viennese is evident and undisputed. An intriguing possibility arises, however, from the study of the Moser cabinet and the chronology of major designs by Mackintosh. The Glasgow designer enjoyed far more sympathetic appreciation amongst the artists of Vienna than among his own countrymen. The question is posed of the extent to which the exchange of ideas between Mackintosh and the Secessionists was reciprocal. In this context, the Moser cabinet makes a fascinating comparison with the white cabinet designed by Mackintosh in 1902 (Fig. 3), sold by Sotheby's in 1984. Both have doors designed to fold back and are decorated on the inside panels with stylised, symbolist female figures. Mackintosh must have seen Moser's design, as a fellow exhibitor in 1900, and it is interesting to speculate whether the Viennese piece influenced him in the germination of his own masterpiece. Moser's cabinet tells us a great deal of the story of design at the turn of the century in Vienna, whilst preserving a subtle sense of mystery.

Fig. 2
A Secessionist ivory, mother-of-
pearl, ebony, elm and jacaranda-
inlaid desk designed by Koloman
Moser, Vienna, 1902,
width 3ft 11¼in (120cm)

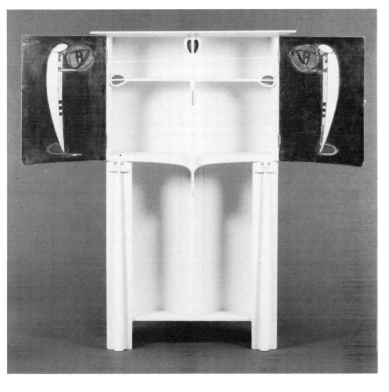

Fig. 3
A painted wood cabinet decorated with
coloured-glass mosaic on panels of silver leaf,
designed by Charles Rennie Mackintosh, 1902,
height 5ft 1in (154.8cm)

# Jewellery

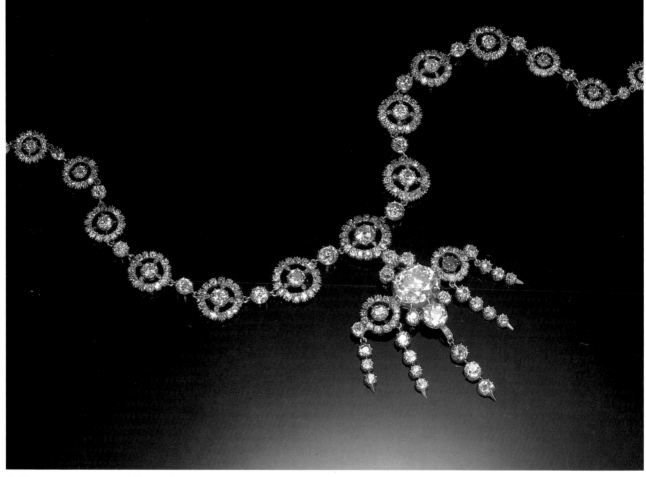

A diamond necklace, eighteenth century, with a pink diamond pendant, nineteenth century
London £209,000 ($267,520). 23.V.85

A diamond rivière, *circa* 1820
London £148,500 ($190,080). 23.V.85
From the collection of the Marquess of Conyngham

According to family tradition, this necklace was presented by George IV to his mistress Elizabeth,
Lady Conyngham

An emerald and diamond brooch, nineteenth century, SFr 1,210,000 (£365,559 : $467,181)
An emerald and diamond pendant, nineteenth century, SFr 374,000 (£112,991 : $144,402)

The jewellery illustrated on this page is from the collection of the late King Umberto II of Italy and was sold in Geneva on 15 May 1985.

*Opposite, clockwise from left to right*
An alexandrite, half-pearl and diamond brooch-pendant, last quarter nineteenth century, £29,700 ($38,016)
A gold and sapphire brooch by Castellani, *circa* 1860, £1,980 ($2,534)
A gold, enamel and jewelled Holbeinesque pendant, *circa* 1870, £4,950 ($6,336)
A gold, enamel and jewelled necklace and pendant by Giuliano, *circa* 1890, £5,720 ($7,322)
A gold, enamel and sapphire pendent cross by Giuliano, *circa* 1900, £660 ($845)

The jewellery illustrated on the page opposite was sold in London on 23 May 1985

An emerald and diamond necklace
New York $308,000 (£240,625). 18.X.84

A ruby and diamond necklace by Ostertag
New York $572,000 (£446,875). 23.IV.85

From the collection of Annie-Laurie Aitken

An Art Deco chinoiserie mystery clock by Cartier, 1928, supported by a jade elephant,
eighteenth century, height 7⅝in (19.5cm)
Geneva SFr440,000 (£132,931 : $169,884). 15.V.85

*Opposite*
An Art Deco coral and rock crystal mystery clock by Cartier, *circa* 1928, height 5⅛in (13cm)
St Moritz SFr176,000 (£53,172 : $67,954). 23.II.85

A cultured pearl necklace
New York $198,000 (£154,688). 23.IV.85

*Opposite*
A turquoise and diamond demi-parure by Bulgari, comprising a necklace, a brooch-pendant, a pair
of earrings and a single unmounted turquoise
St Moritz SFr 92,400 (£27,915 : $35,676). 23.II.85

An emerald and diamond cross-over ring, SFr57,200 (£17,281:$22,085)
A pair of emerald and diamond pendent earrings, SFr27,500 (£8,308:$10,618)
An emerald and diamond necklace with detachable pendant, SFr50,600 (£15,287:$19,537)
An Art Deco platinum and diamond bracelet by Cartier, 1928, SFr374,000 (£112,991:$144,402)

The jewellery illustrated on this page was sold in St Moritz on 23 February 1985

An Art Deco diamond, rock crystal and enamel brooch by Cartier, *circa* 1925, $8,800 (£6,875)
An Art Deco platinum, fancy colour diamond and black onyx necklace by Cartier, *circa* 1925,
$60,500 (£47,266)
An alexandrite and diamond cluster ring, *circa* 1900, $10,450 (£8,164)
An Art Deco fancy yellow diamond and black onyx ring by Cartier, *circa* 1925, $16,500 (£12,891)

The jewellery illustrated on this page is from the Estate of Amelia Peabody and was sold in New York
on 22 April 1985

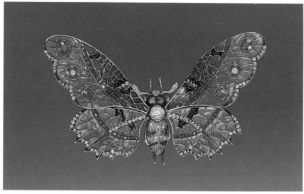

An emerald-cut diamond
(18.42 carats) ring
New York $451,000
(£352,344). 23.IV.85

From the collection of
Annie-Laurie Aitken

An Art Nouveau *plique-à-jour* enamel and jewelled
butterfly brooch, *circa* 1900
Geneva SFr 77,000 (£23,263 : $29,730). 15.XI.84

A diamond (25.15 carats)
ring by Harry Winston
St Moritz SFr 2,310,000
(£697,885 : $891,892).
23.II.85

*Left to right*
An oval-shaped fancy pink diamond (5.07 carats) ring
New York $231,000 (£180,469). 5.XII.84

A heart-shaped diamond (23.31 carats) pendant
New York $660,000 (£515,625). 5.XII.84

The 'Punch Jones' diamond (34.46 carats)
New York $74,250 (£58,008). 18.X.84

*Left to right*
An emerald-cut fancy blue diamond (12.22 carats) ring
by Harry Winston
New York $990,000 (£773,438). 23.IV.85

A cabochon sapphire (24.53 carats) and diamond ring
New York $231,000 (£180,469). 13.VI.85

A cushion-shaped ruby and diamond ring
New York $297,000 (£232,031). 23.IV.85

*Opposite*
An emerald and diamond choker-necklace, $41,800 (£32,656)
An emerald and diamond brooch by Van Cleef & Arpels, $93,500 (£73,047)
An emerald and diamond bracelet by Van Cleef & Arpels, $115,500 (£90,234)
An emerald and diamond ring by Van Cleef & Arpels, $44,000 (£34,375)

The jewellery illustrated on the page opposite is from the Estate of Jeanne E. Kerbs and was sold in
New York on 18 October 1984.

A pair of platinum and diamond earrings by David Webb, $24,200 (£18,906)
A sapphire and diamond necklace with a detachable pendant by Cartier, *circa* 1915,
$70,400 (£55,000)
A cabochon sapphire (13.00 carats) and diamond ring, $13,200 (£10,313)

The jewellery illustrated on this page is from the collection of Françoise and Oscar de la Renta and
was sold in New York on 13 June 1985

An emerald and diamond bracelet by Tiffany & Co., *circa* 1925, $143,000 (£111,719)
An emerald-cut emerald (9.21 carats) and diamond ring, $104,500 (£81,641)
An emerald (5.67 carats) and diamond brooch, $33,000 (£25,781)
An emerald and diamond ring by Van Cleef & Arpels, $29,700 (£23,203)

The jewellery illustrated on this page is from the collection of Annie-Laurie Aitken and was sold in
New York on 23 April 1985

# Antiquities and Asian art

A Phoenician ivory plaque, Arslan Tash, north Syria, ninth-eighth century BC,
4in by 3in (10.1cm by 7.7cm)
London £30,800 ($39,424). 17.VII.85
From the collection of Christopher Terry

This plaque probably came from a piece of furniture in the palace of Arslan Tash. The subject, traditionally termed the 'woman at the window', has been identified as a cult representation of Ashtart (a Phoenician form of Aphrodite), or her votaress, as a sacred temple prostitute.

An Attic black-figure amphora of Panathenaic form, belonging to Group E, last quarter
sixth century BC, height 12in (30.5cm)
London £22,000 ($28,160). 17.VII.85

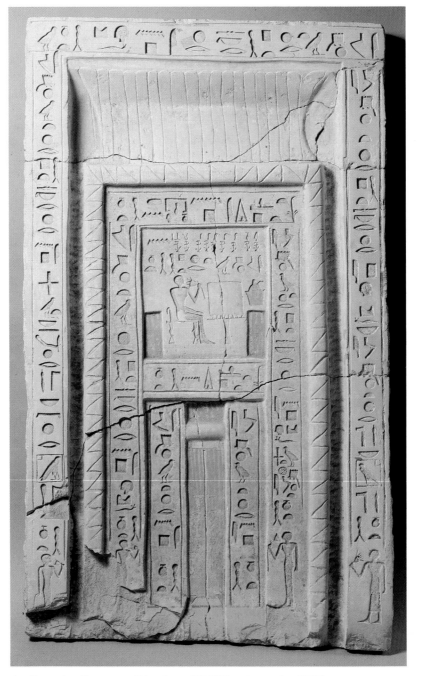

An Egyptian limestone false door, Old Kingdom, *circa* 2200 BC,
43¼in by 25in (109.9cm by 63.5cm)
London £24,200 ($30,976). 10.XII.84

*Opposite*
An Egyptian diorite head of a priest, Thirtieth – Thirty-first Dynasty,
probably reign of Nectanebo II, 360 – 342 BC, height 8in (20.3cm)
New York $93,500 (£73,047). 8.II.85
From the Nadler Collection

A Roman bronze figure of Hermes,
*circa* early second century AD,
height 7¾in (19.7cm)
New York $99,000 (£77,344).
8.II.85

*Opposite*
A Roman marble figure of a woman,
*circa* AD 130–150, height 70¾in (179.8cm)
New York $79,750 (£62,305). 8.II.85

A Khmer sandstone torso of a male deity, Kulen style, ninth century,
height 22⅜in (57cm)
London £20,900 ($26,752). 10.VI.85

A pre-Angkor bronze figure of the Bodhisattva
Avalokitesvara, seventh-eighth century,
height 10⅝in (27cm)
London £20,350 ($26,048). 10.VI.85

A Nepalese gilt-copper figure of Tara,
*circa* fourteenth century, height 6⅞in (17.5cm)
London £7,150 ($9,152). 26.XI.84
From the collection of the Metropolitan Museum of Art,
New York

# Tribal art

A Fang wood female reliquary figure, Gabon,
height 15⅞in (40.5cm)
London £66,000 ($84,480). 24.VI.85

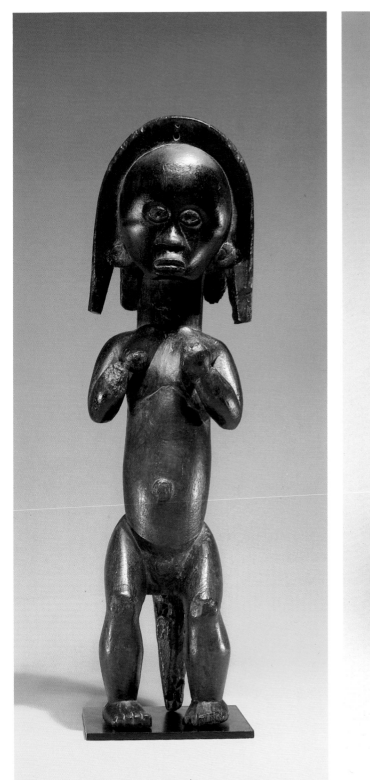

A Fang wood female reliquary figure, Gabon,
height 25⅜in (64.5cm)
New York $77,000 (£60,156). 16.V.85

A Luba Shankadi wood female ancestor figure, Zaire,
height 15½in (39.5cm)
London £20,900 ($26,752). 24.VI.85

A Chinesco terracotta female figure, south-west Nayarit, Protoclassic period, *circa* 100 BC – AD 250, height 16¾in (42.5cm)
New York $37,400 (£29,219). 27.XI.84
From the collection of Alexander Acevedo

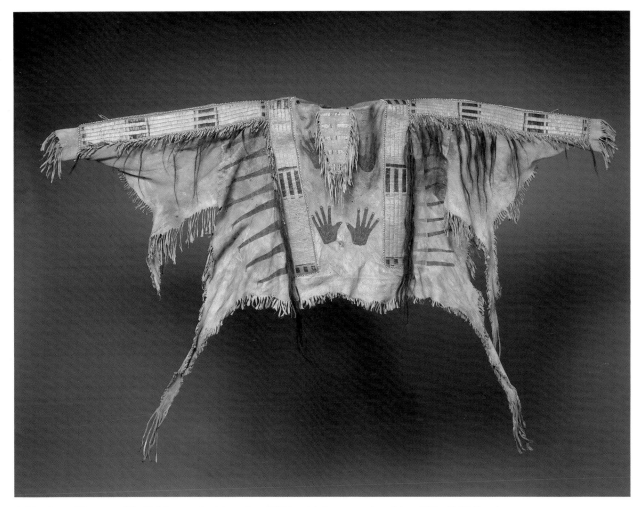

A Yankton Sioux quilled hide man's shirt, *circa* 1867, width across shoulders 68in (172.8cm)
New York $82,500 (£64,453). 25.X.84

# Islamic art

An Ottoman silver-gilt jug, early sixteenth century, height 4in (10.1cm)
London £77,000 ($98,560). 16.IV.85

*Opposite*
A Syrian underglaze-painted pottery jar, late thirteenth–fourteenth century,
height 14⅛in (35.9cm)
London £52,800 ($67,584). 17.X.84

A Mamluk gilt and enamelled glass jug, fourteenth century, height 6⅝in (17cm)
London £29,700 ($38,016). 16.IV.85

A western Persian gold and silver-inlaid brass casket, early fourteenth century, height 5in (12.7cm)
London £42,900 ($54,912). 16.IV.85

A Polonaise silk and metal-thread carpet, seventeenth
century, 13ft 6in by 5ft 9in (410.8cm by 175.4cm)
London £176,000 ($225,280). 17.X.84
From the collection of the late King Umberto II of
Italy

The generic but misleading term 'Polonaise' stems
from the Paris International Exhibition of 1878,
when a silk pile and metal-thread carpet of this type
belonging to a Polish family was exhibited. From a
series of erroneous assumptions it was presumed that
all such carpets were Polish. The carpets were, in
fact, among the most luxurious products of the Persian
court factories of the Safavid period, and served
ideally as diplomatic gifts to European monarchs
and ambassadors.

*Opposite*
A Polonaise silk and metal-thread rug, seventeenth
century, 6ft 9in by 4ft 5in (205.8cm by 134.7cm)
London £198,000 ($253,440). 17.X.84
From the collection of the late King Umberto II of
Italy

A Heriz silk rug, *circa* 1875, 6ft 1in by 4ft 7in (185.5cm by 139.8cm)
New York $51,700 (£40,391). 18.V.85

A Kum Kapour prayer rug, signed by Zare, *circa* 1903 –1906, 4ft by 2ft 9in
(122cm by 83.8cm)
New York $60,500 (£47,266). 18.V.85

A Salor silk and wool chuval, first half nineteenth century, 2ft 10in by 4ft 6in (86.4cm by 137.2cm)
New York $23,100 (£18,047). 1.XII.84

A Saryk carpet, *circa* 1800, 6ft 11in by 6ft 7 in (211cm by 200.8cm)
New York $24,200 (£18,906). 18.V. 85

# Chinese art

A pair of *sancai* glazed pottery figures of earth spirits, Tang Dynasty,
heights 36in and 37½in (91.5cm and 95.2cm)
New York $193,600 (£151,250). 3.XII.84
From the Schloss Collection

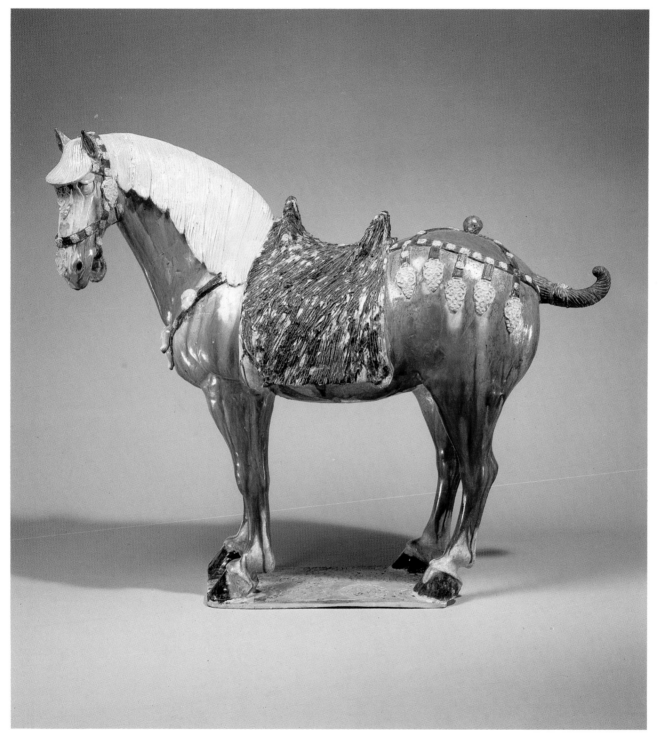

A *sancai* glazed pottery figure of a horse, Tang Dynasty, height 26½in (67.2cm)
New York $660,000 (£515,625). 3.XII.84
From the Schloss Collection

A Dingyao tripod censer, Song Dynasty, diameter 5in (12.7cm)
London £45,100 ($57,728). 11.XII.84

*Opposite*
A Junyao flowerpot, Song Dynasty, diameter 11⅛in (28.2cm)
Hong Kong HK $1,210,000 (£121,000:$155,727). 21.V.85
From the collection of the J.T. Tai Foundation

A pair of Ming blue and white bowls, Jiajing, diameter 6½in (16.5cm)
New York $203,500 (£158,984). 4.VI.85
From the J.M. Hu Family Collection

A Ming blue and white dish, Yongle, diameter 14$\frac{7}{8}$in (37.7cm)
Hong Kong HK $902,000 (£90,200:$116,088). 19.XI.84
From the collection of the late Dr Ip Yee

*Opposite*
Two views showing the top and bottom of a Ming polychrome box and cover, Jiajing,
width 6$\frac{1}{4}$in (15.8cm)
New York $132,000 (£103,125). 4.VI.85
From the J.M. Hu Family Collection

A pair of Ming figures of immortals, Wanli, heights 17¾in and 17⅛in (45cm and 43.5cm)
London £68,200 ($87,296). 18.VI.85

A Ming polychrome wine jar and cover, Jiajing, height $17\frac{7}{8}$in (45.5cm)
New York $1,210,000 (£945,313). 4.VI.85
From the J.M. Hu Family Collection

A pair of Imperial *famille rose* vases, Qianlong, height 7¾in (19.7cm)
London £418,000 ($535,040). 18.VI.85

A celadon-ground *famille rose* moonflask, Qianlong, height 10½in (26.7cm)
Hong Kong HK $1,485,000 (£148,500:$191,120). 21.V.85
From the collection of the J.T. Tai Foundation

An export *famille rose* basin, Qianlong, probably after a design by Cornelius Pronck,
diameter 18¾in (47.6cm)
London £35,200 ($45,056). 20.XI.84

*Opposite, above*
A pair of cloisonné enamel ewers, Qianlong, height 12¼in (31.1cm)
London £38,500 ($49,280). 2.XI.84

*Opposite, below*
A lacquer folding table, seventeenth century, diameter 5ft (153cm)
London £10,450 ($13,376). 2.V.85

A sandstone figure of Buddha,
Tang Dynasty, height 26in (66cm)
New York $220,000 (£171,875).
3.VI.85
From the collection of the J.T. Tai
Foundation

*Opposite*
A stone Buddhist votive stele,
Wei Dynasty, first half sixth century,
height 55½in (141cm)
London £242,000 ($309,760).
18.VI.85

**Zheng Xie**
BAMBOO AND ROCKS
Hanging scroll, ink on paper, signed, with four seals of the artist, inscribed
with a poem and dated 1760, 66in by 40⅜in (167.6cm by 102.5cm)
Hong Kong $209,000 (£20,900:$26,898). 21.XI.84
From the collection of the late Dr Ip Yee

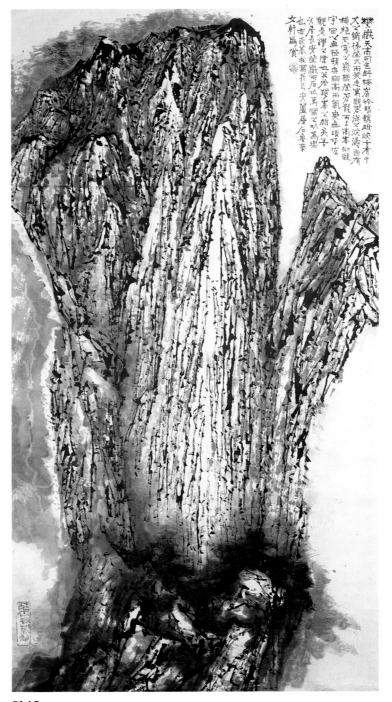

**Shi Lu**
HUASHAN
Hanging scroll, ink on paper, signed and dated 1971, 59in by 31¾in
(150cm by 80.6cm)
New York $57,200 (£44,688). 3.VI.85

**Sudan Xie**
DAODE JING
A manuscript fragment, handscroll, ink on paper, signed and dated AD 270,
12⅛in by 82in (30.8cm by 208.3cm)
New York $90,750 (£70,898). 3.VI.85

**Wen Zhengming**
RIVER LANDSCAPE
Handscroll, ink on paper, signed, with two seals of the artist and dated 20 October 1499,
$6\frac{7}{8}$in by $49\frac{1}{4}$in (17.5cm by 125cm)
New York $187,000 (£146,094). 5.XII.84

This is believed to be the earliest known dated work of Wen Zhengming.

# The Mottahedeh Collection
# of Chinese export porcelain

David S. Howard

At the auction of any great private collection it is not only the works of art that are put to the test: the judgement of the collector, the fame of the collection, the extent to which it has become a published record, as well as the work of the auctioneer, particularly before the sale, are all tested inexorably. It is impossible to put an exact value on each factor and this makes prices unpredictable, but when a selection of almost half of the Mottahedeh Collection was sold by Sotheby's, New York, at the end of January, they all played a part in raising the reputation of Chinese export art in general and providing a considerable number of records in particular.

The collection had been acquired over a fifty-year period, often at prices of an earlier age. It was formed in the two lifetimes of Rafi and Mildred Mottahedeh of New York, who had constantly stepped beyond current scholarship to make new discoveries and, with a genius not always associated with collectors, assembled the widest ranging selection of pieces to provide a full history of the subject. The collection was duly published by Sotheby Parke Bernet Publications in 1978 as *China for the West* and has become a reference point for many students, sales catalogues and subsequent exhibitions.

For those, not least Mildred Mottahedeh, who after Rafi's death had agonised over the dispersal of such a unique assemblage, the fact that the pieces were all illustrated, recorded and analysed made their physical presence together of less importance and it was decided, in the words of Edmond de Goncourt in his will of 1897, that they were to be 'dispersed under the auctioneer's hammer so that the delight I had in acquiring them should be repaid, through each of them, to an inheritor of my tastes'.

An unusual feature of such an important sale of export ware was the lack of pieces more notable for their decorative than for their documentary or historic value. This was well illustrated by armorial porcelain, which sold exceptionally well. On the other hand, some of the forms that the Mottahedehs collected as examples of the influence of the European market, urns, vases, tureens and figures, whose main purpose today is decorative, did not reach the same price level at this sale (Fig. 1).

Fig. 1
A pair of export figures of French courtiers, *circa* 1700–1715, heights 9in and 8⅞in
(22.8cm and 22.5cm)
New York $20,900 (£16,328). 30.I.85
From the Mottahedeh Collection

Fig. 2
An export *famille rose* and grisaille punch bowl, with a view showing the Mansion House, London,
*circa* 1802, diameter 15¾in (40cm)
New York $19,800 (£15,469). 30.I.85
From the Mottahedeh Collection

Fig. 4
An export charger with a *famille rose* border, *circa* 1740, diameter 14in (35.5cm)
New York $12,650 (£9,883). 30.I.85
From the Mottahedeh Collection

*Opposite*
Fig. 3
An export *famille rose* punch bowl, 1745–55, diameter 16in (40.6cm)
New York $29,700 (£23,203). 30.I.85
From the Mottahedeh Collection

The decorative value of Chinese export porcelain was never the prime consideration for the Mottahedehs. In addition to their specific aim of providing material for research, they also occasionally bought a piece as a pattern for their internationally successful porcelain-making enterprise. They lost count of the times that in the early days their own reproductions had been offered to them as genuine antiques by hopeful dealers, something which caused them to mark their reproductions in a way that made it impossible to remove their marks, even by grinding, as had been achieved on some of their early pieces.

The success of the sale, which made over $1 million, testified to the rarity of much of the export porcelain. Even where there was considerable damage, this did not influence the price if the item was of real interest. Thus, a shaped blue armorial basin with the arms of Da Costa sold for $9,075, in spite of a reconstructed section of the rim, and the decoratively excellent bowl with two scenes of London reached $19,800 (Fig. 2), despite many repairs.

It was always the European scenes on dinner services that most excited our eighteenth-century forebears and these have remained firm favourites since. The Mottahedeh Collection was particularly rich on this score and Don Quixote and Andromeda jostled with Harlequin and Hercules on plates, cups, salts, a Toby ale jug and punch bowls, bringing some exceptional prices in the mêlée. Among the punch bowls was a rare piece with a scene of seventeenth-century horsemen (Fig. 3). A dish with a Dutch scene of a skating lesson after Cornelius Dusart (Fig. 4) sold well while a plate with a view of Amsterdam, well known from the reproduction piece by the Metropolitan Museum, New York, sold for $6,325. Six plates painted after the Italian Comedy provided no surprise at $31,900 for the set. A cup and saucer painted after Cornelius Pronk with a scene known as 'The doctor's visit' sold well for $5,280 and a plate with a European scene 'In the arbour' even better at $7,975. (Neither were as unusual, or in my opinion as interesting, as the Pronk wall sconce, which reached $6,050). Among the religious scenes the 1750 *famille rose* 'Ascension' at $6,050 must have been easily the most expensive plate in a service.

When the Dutch East India Company merchants had surprised and delighted their European clients for half a century with dinner services, vases, and garnitures, they followed the idea, pioneered at Meissen, of animal figures and well-known historical characters. A tall figure of a Dutch lady, *circa* 1735, who used to be called Lady Duff, at $18,700 did rather better than the more distinguished but smaller pair of *famille verte* figures, said to be Louis XIV with Madame de Maintenon, or de Montespan (neither would have claimed the likeness) (Fig. 1). It was an exciting but motley crew, which included export figures of an owl, a goat, a tortoise tureen and a damaged pair of hefty mid-nineteenth century elephants.

But what was perhaps the rarest and most historically curious lot of all was not even made in China. This was a magnificent set of fourteen engravings of *The conquests of the Emperor Qianlong* (Fig. 5). The original set of sixteen engravings was

Fig. 5
**Jean-Philippe Le Bas after Giuseppe Castiglione**
THE EMPEROR GIVES A VICTORY BANQUET FOR THE DISTINGUISHED OFFICERS AND SOLDIERS
1775, approximately $22\frac{1}{2}$in by $36\frac{1}{2}$in (57.2cm by 92.7cm)

One of an assembled set of fourteen from a complete set of sixteen engravings of *The Conquests of the Emperor Qianlong, circa* 1770–75
New York $29,700 (£23,203). 30.I.85
From the Mottahedeh Collection

commissioned by the Emperor in 1765 for the central hall of his palace of Beijin. The drawings for the project were prepared in China by four Jesuits under their director Giuseppe Castiglione. These were sent to France where the work was completed by eight engravers under the direction of Charles-Nicolas Cochin of the Académie Royale at the court of Louis XVI. The copper plates and 200 copies of each engraving were returned to China but none appear to have survived. Of the few copies that remained in France, sets are known at the Musée Guimet, the Bibliothèque Mazarin, the Bibliothèque Nationale in Paris and at the Château de Coppet in Switzerland, the gift of Louis XIV to Necker. This only Western lot among 374 Oriental pieces, which sold for $29,700, was perhaps the most spectacular of all, although it will be the kaleidoscope of history, enterprise and craftsmanship that will long be remembered rather than the prices.

# Japanese art

A Namban lacquer shrine, Momoyama period (1573–1615), height 16in (40.7cm)
New York $165,000 (£128,906). 11.IV.85

A lacquer *kago* (ceremonial palanquin), Edo period (1615–1868), height 54⅛in (137.5cm)
London £26,400 ($33,792). 31.X.84

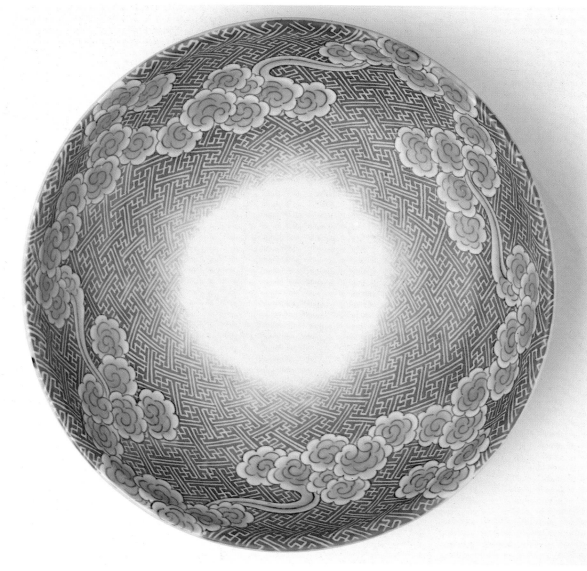

A Nabeshima dish, eighteenth century, diameter 12in (30.6cm)
London £31,900($40,832). 6.III.85

pair of Arita figures of eagles, late seventeenth century, heights $21\frac{1}{8}$in and $20\frac{5}{8}$in
.6cm and 52.5cm)
ndon £55,000($70,400). 13.VI.85

A gold lacquer cabinet, Meiji period (1868–1912), height 44½in (113cm)
London £71,500 ($91,520). 31.X.84

This cabinet was given to the Prince of Wales by Crown Prince Hirohito in 1921.

*Opposite*
Six of a set of twelve lacquer zodiac *inro* with *inrobako* by Jokasai, signed, Meiji period (1868–1912)
New York $60,500 (£47,266). 11.IV.85
From the collection of Gretchen Kroch Kelsch

A wood *netsuke* of two monkeys by
Toyomasa, signed, Tamba, early
nineteenth century
London £33,000 ($42,240).
24.X.84
From the collection of
Martin S. Newstead

An ivory *netsuke* of a *baku*, unsigned,
Kyoto, eighteenth century
London £5,940 ($7,603). 14.VI.85

An ivory *manju* by
Kaigyokusai Masatsugu, signed,
Osaka, nineteenth century
London £13,200 ($16,896).
24.X.84

An ivory *netsuke* of a bitch and pup by
Tomotada, signed, Kyoto,
eighteenth century
London £19,800 ($25,344). 24.X.84
From the Collection of Martin
S. Newstead

A wood *netsuke* of an *oshidori* by Masanao,
signed, Kyoto, late eighteenth century
London £48,400 ($61,952). 24.X.84
From the collection of Martin S.
Newstead

*Above, left*
A Satsuma earthenware jar and cover by Chin Jukan, signed *Satsuma kuni, Ishuin Naeshirogawa,*
*Chin Jukan sei,* Meiji period (1868–1912), height 30¼in (77cm)
London £12,650($16,192). 13.VI.85

*Above, right*
A Satsuma earthenware vase by Katsura Chikuso, signed, late Edo period (1803–68),
height 36¼in (92cm)
London £10,450 ($13,376). 13.VI.85

A *plique-à-jour* vase, Meiji period (1868–1912),
height 7⅞in (20cm)
London £6,380($8,166). 13.VI.85

*Opposite, left*
**Ando Hiroshige**
THE KISO GORGE IN SNOW WITH THE FUJI RIVER
Double *oban kakemono-e*, 29in by 9⅜in
(73.8cm by 23.8cm)
New York $12,650 (£9,883). 9.XI.84
From the collection of Charles Hovey Pepper

*Opposite, right*
**Ando Hiroshige**
THE MONKEY BRIDGE IN KOSHU PROVINCE
Double *oban kakemono-e*, 28⅜in by 9¾in
(72.1cm by 24.8cm)
New York $29,700 (£23,203). 9.XI.84
From the collection of Charles Hovey Pepper

A cloisonné enamel vase by Hayashi Kodenji,
signed *Aichi*, *Hayashi ko*, Meiji period
(1868–1912) height 12¼in (31cm)
London £9,900($12,672). 13.VI.85

# The Bermuda postmaster's stamp

Richard Ashton

William Bennet Perot (1791–1871) was postmaster of Hamilton, Bermuda, from 1818 to 1862. His portrait (Fig. 1) still hangs in his former home, Par-le-Ville, which is now the public library of Bermuda. Adjacent is the little post office where, in 1861, philatelic history was, literally, made.

At that time letters for local delivery were taken to the post office and hand-stamped with an impression of the office date-stamp. When the post office was closed, provision was made for letters to be left with the fee of one penny for later delivery. It appears, however, that local residents were often remiss in leaving their pennies, thus defrauding the postmaster who was unable to prove who had or had not left the correct payment. This was a matter for concern since from 1818 the postmasters had been permitted to retain for themselves all monies paid for the delivery of inland mail.

By 1848 the fraud had reached such proportions that Perot, no doubt taking note of the action of American postmasters, decided to issue his own stamps, which could be purchased in advance. Between 1848 and 1856, Perot used the office date-stamp, with the month and day plugs removed, to create his stamps, applying it to sheets of paper that were then cut into squares ready for use. In 1861 a new type was made, using a hand-stamp consisting of a crowned circle with *PAID AT HAMILTON BERMUDA* in the centre. Impressions were struck in red on blue laid paper and, until recently, only four examples were recorded.

The first was discovered in December 1945, still affixed to the original local letter; it was last sold at the dispersal of the Sir Henry Tucker Collections of Bermuda. Second and third examples, both off cover, were discovered by M.H. Ludington in 1948; some years later Mr Ludington acquired the original envelope from which one of these stamps had been removed and, happily, they are now reunited. The fourth, also off cover, was discovered in Bermuda in 1966. All four examples are on the same type of blue laid paper with the customary manuscript *X* cancellation in black ink.

During a postage stamp advisory day at Sotheby's office in Copenhagen, Denmark, a fifth and unused example of the Perot second-type stamp was brought in and identified (Fig. 2). On 14 March 1985 this great rarity was the highlight of a postage stamp auction held by Sotheby's in London, where it was sold for £36,300. Prior to the sale, an American dealer of international repute remarked that the Perot stamp was perhaps the most remarkable philatelic discovery this century.

Fig. 1
William Bennet Perot, postmaster of Hamilton,
Bermuda, 1818–62
Reproduced courtesy of the Bermuda Public Library

Fig. 2
**Bermuda**, 1861 1d carmine on blue laid paper,
unused, prepared by W.B. Perot at Hamilton
London £36,300 ($46,464). 14.III.85

# Postage stamps

**Rhodesia**, 1913–22 double working plate, Head Die III, perforated fourteen, 5d black and pale green, unused horizontal marginal strip of three with the first three vertical rows of perforations omitted London £5,060 ($6,477). 28.XI.84

**Canada**, 1852–57, 3d red on thin soft ribbed paper, unused vertical marginal pair with part inscription London £5,060 ($6,477). 14.III.85

**Rhodesia**, 1913–22 single working plate, perforated fifteen, 1d carmine-red, unused horizontal pair, imperforate between London £6,600 ($8,448). 28.XI.84

**Newfoundland**, 1919 First Trans-Atlantic Air Post, 3¢ brown, unused London £6,875 ($8,800). 14.III.85

**Tobago**, 1886–89 provisional surcharge, ½d on 2½d dull blue, unused vertical pair with surcharge omitted on lower stamp London £6,050 ($7,744). 28.XI.84

**Tobago**, 1886–89 provisional surcharge, ½d on 2½d dull blue, unused vertical pair with surcharge omitted on lower stamp and top with variety 'figure further from word' London £14,850 ($19,008). 28.XI.84

**Tobago**, 1891–92 provisional surcharge, 2½d on 4d grey, unused vertical pair, the top stamp with double surcharge London £1,540 ($1,971). 28.XI.84

**Tobago**, 1886–89 provisional surcharge, ½d on 6d stone, unused vertical pair with surcharge inverted on lower stamp and top stamp with variety 'figure further from word' London £3,300 ($4,224). 28.XI.84

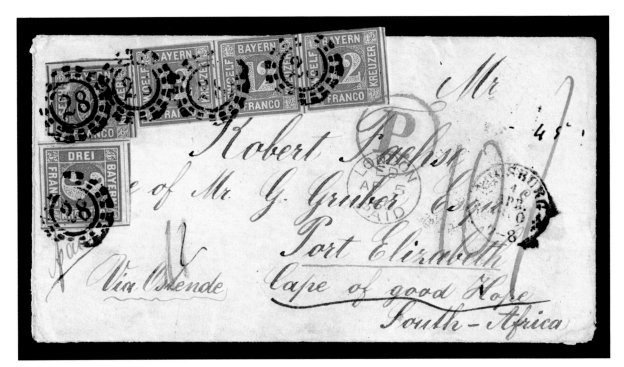

**New South Wales**, 1851 part of a folded letter from Kempsey to France via Sydney,
bearing 2d and 3d 'Sydney view'
London £2,860 ($3,661). 14.III.85

**Bavaria**, 1860 envelope from Augsburg to Port Elizabeth via the Cape of Good Hope, bearing
3 kreuzer, 6 kreuzer and strip of three 12 kreuzer
Johannesburg R4,400 (£1,719:$2,211). 16.IV.85

# Collectors' sales

An English boxwood and ivory miniature ship diorama, early nineteenth century,
width 5⅞in (15cm)
London £12,100 ($15,488). 5.VI.85

A Flemish brass planispheric astrolabe by
Jacobus Valerius, signed, *circa* 1560,
diameter 8⅛in (20.6cm)
London £37,400 ($47,872). 11.VI.85

A compendium microscope by Benjamin
Martin, London, *circa* 1770,
height 13in (33cm)
London £9,350 ($11,968). 20.II.85

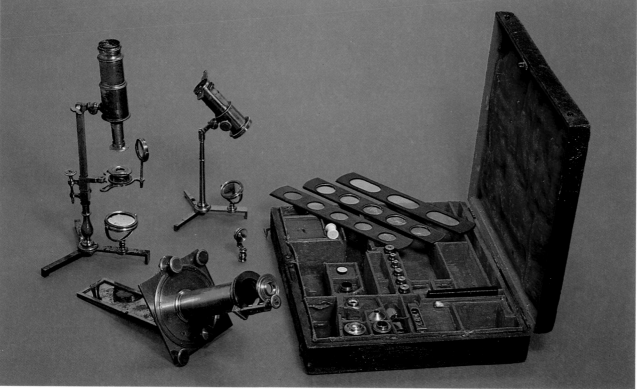

A French musical automaton of a mandolin player
by Gaston Vichy, *circa* 1880, height 33⅛in (84cm)
London £11,880 ($15,206). 23.I.85

A German character doll by Kammer and Reinhardt, the
bisque head incised *K*R 10755, circa* 1910, height 22in (56cm)
London £10,450 ($13,376). 21.V.85

A cut velvet coat and breeches, worn by William James,
The Black Rod of Ireland, 1751
London £13,700 ($17,536). 9.V.85

Now in the Ulster Museum, Northern Ireland

A French doll by Jumeau, the bisque head incised *E.9 J*,
height 20in (50.8cm)
New York $7,975 (£6,230). 29.VI.85

An American cast-iron revolving monkey cage by Hubley, *circa* 1919–26, length 16in (40.7cm)
New York $19,800 (£15,469). 13.IV.85
From the collection of Raymond E. Holland

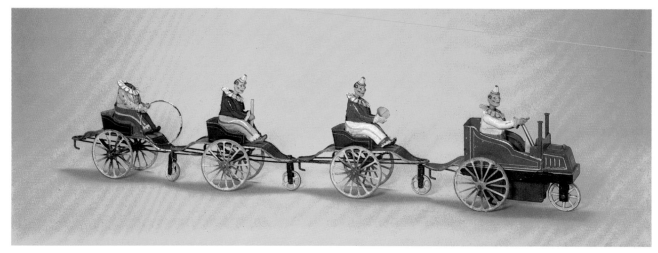

A German tinplate 'Fidelitas' clown car train by Marklin, *circa* 1909, length 37in (94cm)
London £9,900 ($12,672). 21.V.85

John Lennon's psychedelic 1965 Rolls-Royce Phantom V, with bodywork by Mulliner Park Ward
New York $2,299,000 (£1,796,094). 29.VI.85

John Lennon of *The Beatles* bought this car in 1966 and had it painted in 1967, in collaboration with
a mystic friend. It was used by the group until 1969.

# British folk art

## Francesca Mills

When Beatrix Rumford, director of the Abby Aldrich Rockefeller Folk Art Collection in Williamsburg, visited England only a few years back, she looked around museums to find the British equivalent of American folk art. Nobody knew what it was she was looking for. As recently as ten years ago, few people collected British folk art and those who did seem to have been guided largely by an instinctive understanding and discrimination. Enthusiasm for its counterpart, American folk art, has been stimulated by museums and collectors over the last fifty years, yet it is only comparatively recently that a broader awareness of British folk art has begun to emerge, as marked by the first sale devoted to the subject at Sotheby's this summer.

Naïve, primitive, amateur, provincial, popular, vernacular, or self-taught, not one of these terms alone conveys adequately a description of folk art; read together they suggest its essence. It was the work of those without formal training, the art of the common man, covering a wide spectrum of forms and with charms that have little to do with established art criteria. In the absence of the patronage extended to the fine arts, which discriminated against vernacular art altogether, and with the changing circumstances brought about by the Industrial Revolution, both the need for the items and the desire to create them largely came to an end by the mid-nineteenth century, as machines increasingly displaced the skill of craftsman.

Family portraits, domestic and livestock studies, together with sporting and village scenes as diverse as cricket matches and hunting (Fig. 1), rat-catching or bear-bating were subjects to be recorded. The paintings are frequently anonymous and are characterised by simple compositions, painted in broad flat areas of colour. Unusual among folk painters was Tim Bobbin, in reality one John Collier of Lancashire (1708–86), for not only is his name recorded but his work was remarkable. The son of a curate, Collier became an itinerant schoolteacher, eventually taking the post of master of Milnrow School, near Rochdale. He developed a reputation as a painter, engraver and writer, but became fascinated by caricature and turned his talents to producing grotesque representations of dental and medical subjects. A painting in the sale entitled *Temptation* is related to an engraving made for his *Human Passions Delineated* (1772–73) and portrays a scene in which a gentleman is forced to drink a concoction by a leering servant.

Seemingly disproportionate anatomy is often a characteristic of animal paintings. Farmers would commission portraits of their prize-winning beasts, which were

Fig. 1
**W. Williams**
SIXTEEN PAIRS OF HOUNDS IN A HUNT ON THE SOUTH DOWNS
On panel, signed, inscribed and dated *W. Williams pinx$^t$/1791*, 32$\frac{1}{4}$in by 61in (82cm by 155cm)
London £16,500 ($21,120). 17.VII.85

frequently depicted in such an exaggerated form that one wonders at the degree of verisimilitude between the subject and its representation (Fig. 2). From the early eighteenth century, experimentation with breeds to improve and fatten the stock was practised and this feature, when combined with the often unschooled artist's wish to please his patron, perhaps conspired to produce these curious animals.

Textiles, samplers and quilts, are possibly the only areas of folk art that have long been collected. While many craftsmen and women remained anonymous and un-doubtedly came from the artisan classes, samplers were uniquely the work of the privileged classes and are among the few works that are signed. Embroidered textiles clearly reflect social attitudes, with moral and religious texts interwoven with images of home and family. Included in the sale in July were two samplers from 1824, pain-stakingly worked in silk thread by Eliza Saul aged fourteen, of Leak in Lincolnshire, depicting *Adam and Eve in Happiness* and its companion-piece, *Adam and Eve driven out of Paradise*. Quilts, pieced then quilted in adapted versions of traditional designs, are other wonderful examples of the decorative value of utilitarian objects, transformed into works of art.

Furniture made of oak, elm, ash and fruitwoods, beautifully decorated with sten-cilled and painted patterns, was included in Sotheby's sale. Some craftsmen also

turned their hands to carving educational toys, and the butcher's shop (Fig. 3), made perhaps by a local wheelwright, is a fine example. It was probably intended to be instructive as the detail on the carcasses is very precise, while the inclusion of the cardboard print of the royal arms, the sign of royal patronage, is a delightful touch.

Trade signs and weathervanes made of painted, decorated or moulded metal are other everyday objects that have survived. The former rarely indicated the trade carried out as explicitly as in the case of the universally recognised sign of the pawnbroker, a symbol that originally developed from a reference in the Bible and became part of folk tradition. Weathervanes took various forms; ships, animals, fish or pennants, and most often surmounted churches, or were placed on top of farm buildings. The sale included a fine three-dimensional example of a horse made from hand-moulded copper with its cardinal points still intact (Fig. 4).

From its former obscurity the success of Sotheby's sale has ensured that the variety and richness of British folk art will take its rightful place in the national heritage. The paintings, textiles, utilitarian items, furniture and toys will be regarded as the equal of American folk art, with which is has so much in common.

*Opposite*
Fig. 2
**G.B. Newmarch**
A PAIR OF PRIZE RAMS WITH A FARMER
BESIDE A PEN
Signed and dated *1832*,
20in by 29in (51cm by 73.5cm)
London £4,620 ($5,914). 17.VII.85

*Right*
Fig. 3
A carved and painted model of a
butcher's shop, English,
mid-nineteenth century,
20in by 28in (51cm by 71cm)
London £2,640 ($3,379). 17.VII.85

Fig. 4
A copper weathervane of a
standing horse, English,
mid-nineteenth century,
height 72¾in (185cm)
London £2,530 ($3,238).
17.VII.85

An 1899 Star 3½hp four-seater Vis-à-Vis
London (Honourable Artillery Company) £19,250 ($24,640). 24.VI.85

*Opposite, above*
A 1931 Bentley 4½ litre supercharged drophead coupé, with bodywork by Vanden Plas
London (Honourable Artillery Company) £121,000 ($154,880). 10.XII.84

*Opposite, below*
A 1911 Rolls-Royce 40/50hp Silver Ghost two-seater 'Balloon Car'
London (Honourable Artillery Company) £77,000 ($98,560). 10.XII.84

# The 'Blue Train' Bentley

## Michael Worthington-Williams

Had it been possible for Joel Woolf 'Babe' Barnato to have been present at the Honourable Artillery Company in London on the evening of 10 December 1984, it is likely that he would have viewed the proceedings with a mixture of sardonic humour and some incredulity. The occasion was a sale of historic and classic vehicles, in which the last and most important lot was the 1930 Bentley Speed Six Coupé by J. Gurney Nutting (see opposite), of which Barnato had taken delivery in May 1930. The name of Barnato is irrevocably tied to the fortunes of the original old Cricklewood Bentley company, and in order to appreciate the legend that attaches to the 'Blue Train' Bentley it is necessary to examine the history of Barnato himself.

The story is as romantic as any tale of popular fiction and opens in the East End of London during the last century with the birth of Barnet Isaacs into a poor Jewish family. He later changed his name to Barnato, left Britain to seek his fortune and achieved this ambition in the diamond and gold mines of South Africa.

Joel Woolf 'Babe' Barnato inherited a fortune at the age of two, following his father's mysterious death in 1897, falling overboard from the liner *Scot*. Having earned his captaincy in the Great War, the charming and debonaire Barnato also became known as an accomplished sportsman and a crack shot. His neighbours in Grosvenor Square at this time included Rubin, Kidston and Tim Birkin, all members of the Bentley racing team, known as the 'Bentley Boys'. Since Barnato himself had already excelled in this field at Brooklands, he joined them, later becoming chairman of Bentley Motors and investing in the company. Considered by W.O. Bentley to be the best of his drivers, Barnato won at Le Mans in 1928, 1929 and 1930.

He owned a number of Bentley cars, but the best-remembered of these was the Speed Six GJ 3811. Never able to resist a wager, it was at Cannes in March 1931 that Barnato jokingly asserted that, leaving at the same time, he would be in England driving his Bentley before the crack *Train Bleu*, the Monte-Carlo to London express, had reached Calais. In fact, he reached London before the *Blue Train* reached Calais and won his £100 wager in a feat that encapsulated all the magic of the era, his personality and the success of his previous racing experience. The event later inspired the artist Terence Cuneo to recapture that epic drive in his now famous painting.

Woolf Barnato died in 1948, but his daughter Mrs Barnato-Walker saw the 'Blue Train' Bentley, as it is now universally known, sold for the highest price paid for any vintage car in Britain and for any Bentley at auction anywhere in the world.

A 1930 Bentley Silent Speed Six two-door coupé, with bodywork by J. Gurney Nutting
London (Honourable Artillery Company) £270,600 ($346,368). 10.XII.84

# Wine

A bronze corkscrew,
probably English,
mid-nineteenth century
London £4,620 ($5,914).
29.V.85

An Edwin Cotterill
1842 patent self-adjusting
corkscrew, English
London £2,090 ($2,675).
26.IX.84

Château Mouton Rothschild
1924, CB (an Imperial)
London £9,350 ($11,968).
26.IX.84

In the season ending July 1985, wine sales held by Sotheby's world-wide totalled £2,979,062 ($3,813,199). In addition to the fifteen sales held in London, with two others in Pulborough and Chester, two sales were held in Geneva and two in Johannesburg. The first-ever sale in Tokyo, in conjunction with Seibu, the company's agent in Japan, was a spectacular success and will be repeated in November 1985. Many outstandingly high prices were achieved, although they are not strictly comparable to prices obtained in the United Kingdom, owing to differing trading customs in Japan.

Overall, the market has remained firm. American buyers have been encouraged by the weakness of sterling during part of the year and many of the finest wines have found homes across the Atlantic. Large increases in prices have been seen in certain areas. Vintage port has performed well and at the first major sales of 1982 Cru Classé clarets in February and May, prices substantially exceeded the estimates, resulting in their re-appraisal throughout the trade. The first sale of the season included an important selection of vintages of Château Latour from 1893 to 1959 from the cellars of the Comtes de Beaumont, former proprietors of the château, while in Belgium, Switzerland and France other fine cellars have been discovered.

*Left to right*
A lignum vitae wine cistern, late seventeenth century, height 22⅞in (58cm)
London £4,180 ($5,350). 20.III.85

La Tâche 1953, DRC (one magnum), London £250 ($320). 5.XII.84

Château Pétrus 1961, CB (one bottle), London £605 ($774). 20.III.85

Tokay pre-1790 with the seal of Joseph II of Austro-Hungary (one bottle)
London £572 ($732). 26.IX.84

Château Latour 1926, CB (two bottles), London £319 ($408). 26.IX.84

Significant or record prices were achieved during the year for an exceptionally fine Imperial of Château Mouton Rothschild 1924, the first vintage for which Baron Philippe de Rothschild commissioned an artist to design the label, in this case Jean Carlu; £1,430 ($1,830) was realised for five bottles of Romanée Conti 1959; £1,320 ($1,690) for a dozen bottles of Graham 1945; £5,720 ($7,322) for a dozen bottles Château Latour 1945; £253 ($324) for a bottle of Terrantez 1790. Increasing interest has been shown in collectors' items, such as a rare wine cistern in lignum vitae, one of only four recorded examples from the seventeenth century, and an auction record price was achieved for a mid-nineteenth-century bronze corkscrew in the form of two pairs of putti.

Sotheby's has held eleven wine evenings. In May, amateurs and professionals attended a tasting of ninety-three classed growth clarets of the 1978 vintage, which confirmed the excellence of the year, particularly in Pomerol. Vineyard tours of the Rhône and Burgundy were well supported and more are planned. Sotheby's Publications published *Alsace Wines* by Pamela Vandyke Price, the *Book of California Wine*, in conjunction with the University of California, and Rosemary George's *The Wines of Chablis*, which has won four major awards in 1985.

# 'The British Sporting Heritage'

## Richard Allen

In what has now become an annual event at Sotheby's, the closing of the 1984 season was marked by an imaginative exhibition of sporting art through three centuries, held over four weeks at Christmas in association with the British Field Sports Society.

Heralded by a spectacular arrangement of ten oil paintings by Philip Reinagle (1749–1833) flanking the stairs from the New Bond Street entrance, the exhibition testified to the strong tradition of British sporting painting. The first of four galleries devoted to the event introduced the subject of shooting with a full-length portrait of William Somerville by William Aikman (1682–1731). Himself a crack shot, Somerville was shown alongside a first edition of his poem 'The Chace' (*sic*). Pictures by Gilpin, Dighton, Ibbetson, and Morland, together with works of art, guns, game books, porcelain and furniture all presented a grand pageant of sporting artefacts.

The unsentimentalised splendour of Landseer's *Monarch of the Glen* dominated the north gallery, devoted to the theme of stalking and deer hunting. But it was fox-hunting, one of the most popular pursuits of the countryside since the 1830s, enjoyed by landlords and tenants alike, that inevitably commanded the greatest number of exhibits. Pictures by Ferneley, Grant, Marshall, Alken, Rowlandson and Munnings recalled an English landscape where the sport took priority during the winter season. Trophies from candelabra to stirrup-cups all formed part of the splendid showcase.

Otter hunting and fishing also had their place as the exhibition moved from the lush countryside to the grassy river-banks. Rods, flies, pictures and accessories, sculpture and literature lined the walls of the exhibition giving way to the oldest of all country sports, coursing and falconry, 'the sport of kings'.

The general sporting section was probably best summarised by the Alscot Park buffet, a massive oak sideboard, designed by Hughes Protat and made by William Cookes of Warwick in 1851. With fantastically carved panels of game birds, hunting scenes and riflery, this enormous piece monopolised one end of the main gallery and was complemented by a hunt table, around which exaggerated memories of the day's events would have been relived.

The illustrated catalogue of the exhibition included an introduction by the President of the British Field Sports Society, Lord Margadale of Islay, with an additional preface to each of the eight main sporting sections. In all, 335 exhibits were generously loaned by 180 members and seen by over 10,000 visitors to Sotheby's galleries.

The main galleries at Sotheby's showing the hunting section of the exhibition with the stalking exhibits in the background.

*Foreground, left to right*
One of a pair of silver candelabra with a pack of hounds at the base, Garrards, London, 1872; a silver model of a fox, London, 1905; a silver centrepiece of a mounted knight and a huntsman with a stag by John Samuel Hunt, London, 1849

*Background, left to right*
*The hunters' chase*, a Mortlake tapestry *circa* 1650; an antler and ivory armchair by Geismar of Wiesbaden, *circa* 1841; *The Hon. Henry Lowther stalking at Ullswater* by Jacob Thompson, 1842; *The Hon. James Murray with a keeper and deer*, *circa* 1824–26, and *The monarch of the Glen* by Sir Edwin Landseer, RA, 1851; *The Bramham Moor hunt at Weeton Whin* and *The Pytchley hounds feeding*, by Sir Alfred Munnings, PRA, both 1928; *Full cry*, one of a set of three by Henry Alken, Snr; *The meet* and *View haloo*, two from a set of four by John Frederick Herring, Snr.

# Notes on contributors

**Professor Chimen Abramsky** has, since 1974, been Goldsmith Professor of Hebrew and Jewish studies at University College, London, and is now Emeritus Professor at London University. He has written extensively on modern Jewish history and Judaic art and is joint author of *Karl Marx and the English Labour Movement* (1965). His other publications include *Two Prague Haggadahs, 1556 & 1606* and he is the editor of *Essays in Honour of E.H. Carr* (1974).

**David S. Howard** has published *Chinese Armorial Porcelain* (1974) and is co-author of *China for the West* (1978). He lectures frequently in America on Chinese porcelain and was guest curator of the New York exhibitions 'New York and the China Trade' (1984) and 'A Pageant of Heraldry in Britain and America' (1984–85). He owns the firm Heirloom & Howard in London.

**Francesca Mills** is an associate of the Crane Gallery, London and has acted as a consultant on folk art. Her book on British and American folk art is to be published in 1986.

**Terence Pepper** joined the staff of the National Portrait Gallery, London, in 1975, having previously qualified as a barrister and as a librarian. He is now the research assistant responsible for the photographs collection and has organised and compiled catalogues for a number of exhibitions including 'E.O. Hoppé' (1978), 'Norman Parkinson' (1981) and 'Howard Coster' (1985).

**Richard Shone** is associate editor of *The Burlington Magazine* where his reviews and articles have appeared since 1975. He has written extensively on the painters of Bloomsbury and has published *Bloomsbury Portraits* (1976), *The Century of Change* (1977), *The Post-Impressionists* (1980) and is currently at work on a study of the portrait in Britain in the past hundred years.

**A. Kenneth Snowman** trained as a painter and still paints. He is chairman of the family firm of Wartski in London and has written extensively on the art of Carl Fabergé. Among his publications are *Eighteenth Century Gold Boxes of Europe* (1966) and *The Art of Carl Fabergé* (1974). In 1979 he organised and wrote the catalogue for the Fabergé exhibition at the Victoria & Albert Museum, London and acted as curator and wrote the catalogue for the exhibition 'Fabergé, Jeweller to Royalty' (1983) at the Cooper Hewitt Museum of the Smithsonian Institution, New York.

**Mary Anne Stevens** was head of the History and Theory of Art Department at the University of Kent before taking up her appointment in 1983 as Head of Education at the Royal Academy of Arts, London. Apart from organising a number of exhibitions, her publications include *Felix Vallotton* (1975) and *Post-Impressionist Graphics* (1980). She has edited and contributed to *Post-Impressionism: Cross-currents in European Art* (1979), *The Orientalists: Delacroix to Matisse – European Painters in North Africa and the Near East* (1984) and *Edward Lear 1812–1888* (1985).

**Edward J. Sullivan** is Associate Professor of Fine Arts, New York University, with a particular interest in Spanish and Latin American art. He is co-author of *Painting in Spain 1650–1700* and wrote *Goya and the Art of His Time*, both 1982. He has also published a monograph on *Claudio Bravo* (1985), while his book on the sculpture of Fernando Botero will be published next year.

**David Enders Tripp** was formerly head of Sotheby's coin and tapestry departments in New York and is the numismatic advisor to the Estate of Jane Brand Allen. He has contributed research to numerous numismatic works including, *Virgil Brand: The Man and His Era* (1983) and wrote the chapter on numismatics in *The Handbook of Etruscan Studies* (1985).

**Michael Worthington-Williams** has, since 1976, been a consultant to Sotheby's department of veteran and vintage vehicles. In addition to editing *Veteran Car* magazine he contributes to a number of specialist publications and is the author of several books on historical motoring subjects. As past vice-president of the Society of Automotive Historians and currently vice-president of the UK Chapter, he also sits on the dating committee of the Veteran Car Club of Great Britain.

---

The following contributors are experts at Sotheby's:

*London*
Richard Allen, Richard Ashton, Margaret Erskine, Philippe Garner and John Somerville.
*New York*
Fanny Mallary and John L. Tancock.

An Iittala glass vase by Tapio Wirkkala, 1946, height 7⅝in (19.5cm)
London £23,100 ($29,568). 29.XI.84
From the collection of Dan Klein

# Index

An American gilt-copper and zinc 'Fair and Warmer' weathervane of a fire engine, probably by
Cushing & White, Waltham, Massachusetts, *circa* 1871, height 31½in (80cm)
New York $24,200 (£18,906). 8.XII.84